Right from the start, Rosetree  spread joy. She doesn't disapp life with enthralling observati ing. Her page-turning memoir captures the feeling, seeking, and *becoming* of a young woman, and the journey of a soul traveling toward enlightenment.

- Amelia Marie Whalen, author, *Everything You've Ever Done: A Memoir of Unconditional Love and Spiritual Discovery*

Could this be a current version of *Alice's Adventures in Wonderland*? Come peek into Rosetree's exploration of what it means to be human. Like Alice, Rose's reflections reveal what we see on a subconscious level, not just consciously. Baby Boomers especially, make sure your seat belt is fastened low and tight.

- Bobby Norfolk, author, *Eye to the Sky: Storytelling on the Edge of Magic*

Rose Rosetree has given us a memoir to inspire spiritual seekers, yet you might also enjoy it just because this tale is so intensely human. Although the author describes a great deal of struggle and emotional pain (viscerally real, actually), you won't come away from these pages with a feeling of victimhood. Instead, how refreshing is this? You'll encounter a compassionate sense of humor and, beneath that, a sense of forgiveness that just might ennoble you. So rare, that alone is one of many reasons to buy this book.

- Rand Greenfield, author, *A Change of Consciousness: A Hippie's Memoir of the Sixties and Beyond*

When you are a spiritual seeker, it's easy to get off track chasing shiny new objects. Thankfully, Rose Rosetree is out there with exceptional clarity, ready to offer her unique and effective systems for personal growth. Her memoir helps you understand why she was driven to make this kind of difference.

Bigger than All the Night Sky is a spiritual jump-starter that will inspire you to remember who you truly are.

- Lori S. Rubenstein, JD, PCC, author, *Forgiveness: Heal Your Past and Find the Peace YOU Deserve*

Thanks to the vivid, heartfelt, present-tense writing in Rose Rosetree's **Bigger than All the Night Sky,** we can easily identify with her stories of awakening to the reality of each new now.

This is a book for those of us who felt a bit different as we grew up and took in the world around us, only to discover later in life that we had a unique path for which we were being prepared.

- Carol K. Walsh, author, *Painting Life: My Creative Journey Through Trauma*

This memoir, written by a world-renowned teacher of deeper perception, is uniquely insightful... Rosetree shares a quirky yet relatable depth of insight. Kudos!"

- Sue Batton Leonard, author, *Gift of a Lifetime: Finding Fulfilling Things in the Unexpected, Sew the Heart and Lessons of Heart & Soul.*

Bigger
Than All
The
Night Sky

THE START OF SPIRITUAL AWAKENING
A MEMOIR

Rose Rosetree

Women's Intuition Worldwide
Sterling, Virginia

Bigger Than All The Night Sky

THE START OF SPIRITUAL AWAKENING — A MEMOIR.

PUBLISHER'S CATALOGING-IN-PUBLICATION

Names: Rosetree, Rose.

Title: Bigger than all the night sky : the start of spiritual awakening : a memoir / Rose Rosetree.

Description: Second edition. | Sterling, VA : Women's Intuition Worldwide, LLC, [2022] | Includes index.

Identifiers: ISBN 9781935214557 | ISBN 9781935214564 (Kindle) | ISBN 9781935214458 (ebook)

Subjects: LCSH: Rosetree, Rose. | Spiritual biography. | Enlightenment (Buddhism) | Spiritual healing. | Self-actualization (Psychology) | Energy medicine. | BISAC: BIOGRAPHY & AUTOBIOGRAPHY / Personal Memoirs. | BIOGRAPHY & AUTOBIOGRAPHY / Women. | BODY, MIND & SPIRIT / Inspiration & Personal Growth.

Classification: LCC BL73.R67 A3 2018 (print) | LCC BL73.R67 (ebook) | DDC 204.092--dc23

ISBN: 978-1-935214-55-7

LCCN: 201

Please direct all correspondence and inquiries to:

Women's Intuition Worldwide, LLC
116 Hillsdale Drive, Sterling, VA 20164-1201
roserosetree@verizon.net
703-450-9514

Visit our website: www.rose-rosetree.com

Dedication

Did you ever wish you could leap right out of this frustrating world

If only you knew somewhere better to go

And how to get there?

Other times, have you wished that you could simply

Feel at home right where you are right now?

Comfortable and deep down happy.

What if both wishes could come true? That won't just happen. Begin your quest.

I dedicate this memoir to outrageous quests like these. Accordingly, in the story to follow, I'll be calling you "Questing Reader." May my quest inspire yours.

Questing Reader, Let's Squeeze In A Few More Advance Reviews

How amazing it is to be brought back more than 50 years to our joy and tribulations in the three years we spent together in a remarkable school! Recalling high school memories of our shared experience so accurately after all these years is fascinating, but even more so is seeing how Rose's memories paint a vivid portrait of her growth through the years to form the gifted person she is today.

- Roderick G. W. Chu, Chancellor Emeritus,
  Ohio Board of Regents

Like Rose, I attended Brandeis in the 1960s. Like her, I studied with Maharishi during the early years of the TM movement. Which makes it all the more impressive to me how Rose has described all this so vividly, and with compelling clarity. Whatever your spiritual path, this is a memoir to inspire you in your search for truth.

- Jonathan Miller, author,
  My Journey in 1970 to Maharishi's India

Treat yourself to this lively book if you have ever felt lost or wondered why you seem to have come into this world with an inexplicable ache. OR if you just want to hear an unskilled empath tell it like it was, before gaining empath skills. Rose Rosetree's delightful memoir is knowing, funny, beautiful, and wise. And most wonderful of all, it is full of love.

- *Rebecca Barry, author, Recipes for a Beautiful Life*

Annotated Contents

Author's Note: Chapter summaries in the preceding listing *won't* be found in this memoir. Why have I included them here? To help browsers like you prior to purchase. Here I've aimed to supply some of the flavor for each chapter.

Acknowledgments

Bev Upshur, you asked me to write this. You said people would be interested. Actually, I'd already first-drafted this memoir seven years before, but was willing to let it languish, like many a book I've privately written just because I needed to.

Despite putting aside many a first-drafted book, I've managed to publish 21 different titles so far, with 44 authorized editions printed in many languages, a dozen languages besides English. Granted, none of these previous books has been so personal. Publishing this particular title was a stretch -- all the more reason for being grateful to my rigorous, yet gentle, editor Dana Wheeler.

Thanks are also due to every single person praised in the following pages, and to my publishers in the U.S. and abroad. Each of you has helped me to become that improbable thing, both a spiritual teacher and a writer.

These days, my life revolves around family, friends, my clients and students, and the Energy Spirituality® experts I've trained. Each of you inspires me, often delighting me as well, and so each of you deserves my acknowledgement here.

In this memoir I've written what I remember, fact-checked it all within reason. Beyond that, no claim is made to perfect reportorial accuracy.

Regarding the memories shared with you here, may the very act of reading all this embolden you, Questing Readers. Since sometimes you need the occasional nudge to trust your own version of what is personally true for you. Inner reality isn't the only truth, but it does matter.

Rose's Photo Gallery

Browse Away!

Find family pictures at
https://www.rose-rosetree.com/books/bigger-than-all-the-night-sky/

You'll also find "Free Tastes"

Supplementing this memoir.

Introduction

Manhattan in 1949 was no longer quite as safe as it had been when my mother and her sisters would *Go Play* in Central Park. Still, it was perfectly fine for Sue Rosenbaum to enjoy a welcome vacation from parenting by sitting in her favorite coffee shop, sipping a leisurely cup of coffee.

At 25, Sue didn't exactly love being stuck at home with her sickly little infant. She really needed a break every weekday: sitting near the big, glass window; taking an occasional peek at the carriage outside that window. Her kid's carriage was safe enough, and thankfully out of earshot for a change.

Besides, her child with the piercing scream was unlikely to cry, not while tucked into her boxy, black baby carriage. That kid really loved being outside in the City.

Always, Sue took her coffee light, with two saccharines. If she felt awkward sitting alone, she could stir her drink a lot, maybe pretending that she — not Lauren Bacall — was the famous movie star who had gone to Julia Richmond High School. Often a friend would keep the young mother company. Otherwise, she'd watch the smoke curling up from her Pall Mall cigarette, since one was always kept in an ashtray, merrily burning away.

Meanwhile, outside the window, Sue could be entertained by the sight of her one-year-old baby. Flirting.

* * *

Questing Reader, I was that baby who just loved when her carriage was parked near the bustling foot traffic of college students. World War II had ended five years before. Now the streets near Columbia University bustled with guys on the GI Bill... and coeds aiming to get their M.R.S. degree.

Soft blankets in my carriage carried the familiar tobacco fragrance of home, yet around me there were so many other smells, each one telling me more about life on earth *now*. This delicious learning was a thrill for me, the biggest thrill imaginable.

My baby's body was developing slowly, far too slowly for impatient little me. At six months old, I could barely hold my head up, and managed to roll over only with considerable effort. Sitting on my own was still too challenging. Yet I was determined to master that eventually, and even learn how to crawl. Meanwhile I'd figured out a fascinating game.

Whenever Mother and I went outside for our city adventures, she always gave me a toy to keep me company in the carriage, my favorite toy, a rattle: formed from crisp plastic, making a comforting sound of click-click-click; entertainingly shaped, with round circles of pastel yellow and green and blue. Felt good. Tasted excellent. Definitely, this was one of my very favorite toys.

Questing Reader, here's what I'd do with my wonderful rattle. I'd hold it in readiness until, from the vantage point of my parked carriage, I could hear the approach of grownups who sounded interesting.

Yes, sounded interesting. Was it possible to tell all the voices apart, learning in advance who was approaching my carriage? Nothing easier!

Granted, my body was slow, but I had a bright, shiny infant's hearing; easily allowing me to untangle the threads of separate voices. Accordingly, I would choose whichever voices sounded most awake, those grownups who could listen the best, the ones who would be able to pick up the gift I was about to bestow, and maybe even pass it forward.

When one of those voices approached, I would spring into action: Pick up my rattle and then, working hard, manage to flip it right out of my carriage; landing my beautiful rattle with a just-right, plastic-type clunk on the pavement.

Soon one of those bright-voiced college grownups would pick it up and offer it back to me, maybe taking a few seconds to play. Prolonging the encounter, I would coo and feel his smile or smell her perfume; sometimes we would play for a very long while; and always I would send out a big burst of joy, the way babies like me know how to do and which, of course, was the whole point of the game.

Maybe I wasn't the best messenger, compared to other babies who had an easier time with their bodies, but I still knew my job. *Bring joy. Bring joy. As much joy as I can bring into this world.*

Why exactly? Pre-birth memories came and went, yet through all the confusions of life, I have always remembered joy best. Therefore, even as a baby who couldn't move very well yet, I knew, "Nothing ever will matter more than this: to bring people those little bursts of joy." A softly spreading, soul-sticky joy, brimming over with connection to All That Is; love as big as a cloudless blue sky when the sun is shining, a mysterious love that people can't photograph or quote or, for that matter, even quite remember.

Isn't every human alive involved in waking up that connection? Questing Reader, the story I'll share with you is about my can't-stop-it groping for truth, even during the years when this felt like a cruel mockery, an endless grope-in-the-dark that turned up nothing.

Unpredictably, at other times, my truth-seeking became pure delight; whether seeking on my own or finding that I had helped others.

Long before concepts like *poking* on Facebook, and even before I could speak out loud; every day that I used to play in my baby carriage; ever since, too — and probably for as long as you've been alive, Questing Reader -- communication would burst out from me, sudden words moving fast-fast-fast. To this day, as an adult, the words that I speak can surprise me as much those who hear them, a spontaneous process that once startled some college kids who never expected to meet me. Taking a stroll near Columbia University, those post-war students would see a colorful rattle zoom out of nowhere, dropping down to fall next to their feet.

PART ONE. Confusions and Delights

CHAPTER 1.

Into the Box

Here's how it starts. I'm gazing downward at the people in this hospital room, enjoying my usual detachment as a soul who still is free to come and go. Often we fetus folks seek relief from womb-time by going Home, returning only when good and ready.

Only now it's dawning on me with a sickening thud that my physical birth is in progress. Quite literally, push will soon come to shove. Looking down from the ceiling, what I see doesn't look good. Sue's toward the end of labor now, sweating and shaking in terror. For once, her short brown hair looks messy, while her big, brown eyes squeeze tightly shut.

Handling her latest contraction, muscles all over Sue's face scrunch up with effort. Cheeks raised, mouth open, she's silently panting, as though clenching her face and her fists could prevent how a certain part of her body happens to be exploding with an entirely new kind of pain.

Feeling physically overwhelmed is unusual for Sue, whose curvy figure disguises a muscular build. Wheeled into the delivery room a few minutes ago, her strong body has quickly progressed into a more active phase of labor. Electrical shocks of spiritual grace are entering through the top of her head like miniature lightning bolts. Sue doesn't notice. If she could, maybe the poor woman wouldn't feel so alone in her physical pain. Although, given her contempt for God, if anyone told her about this particular form of Divine-level comfort, that news might not be especially welcome.

Harsh contractions move Sue's baby outward toward birth, that baby being me; only the inner me is still looking down from the ceiling. Because who in her right mind would move her consciousness in that scared-animal baby body? You kidding? It's far more pleasant, stretching a bit and shifting into my full-sized, gigantic body of light. Hovering close to the ceiling, I definitely prefer to look down and watch my own birth.

Observing my mother, Sue, I feel sorry for her. Not only is the woman physically overwhelmed. When I look closer at her energy, I find that terror is building faster than her physical contractions, and even if the language of Telepathy didn't come so naturally to a baby like me, Sue's fears would register as screamingly loud.

How much more is this going to hurt? Nobody told me how it could hurt so much. This feels like I'm dying. Really, what if I'm going to die now, giving birth?

Or what if my baby is dying, and that's why it hurts so much? Maybe I will die but the baby will live. Which will it be? Which would be worse?

Fears race through Sue's mind, her worries keeping pace with the pain, until her thinking dulls down into a terrified resignation.

Now her relentless contractions come quicker. Less noticeable are the *grace rays* that keep energetically opening up my mother-to-be. Standard human-adult dullness keeps Sue's awareness half-numb. Otherwise, she might feel awe at all the hidden energies helping her to give birth.

What else makes Sue's labor so scary? This war bride's knowledge of childbirth is typical for her generation. She's been taught almost nothing about childbirth, let alone having received an education in energy. Observe this huge sacred light show? Suzanne Audrey Rosenbaum doesn't even own the *concept* of Sacred Light Show.

This hurts like hell. Do other women really have to go through this too, or is my version worse? As usual.

Even from a strictly human perspective, Sue has not been well prepared for childbirth, having been told only this: Labor would come, and it would hurt, but only for a little while -- maybe like menstrual cramps, except a bit worse. Afterward she'd soon forget any pain, forgetting any little pains immediately, soon as she held that beautiful new baby in her arms. And then she would feel the greatest love on earth, a special adoration that every mother automatically feels for her child.

Some menstrual cramps! They lied, that's for sure.

Poor Sue, having nobody to prepare her. What was she supposed to do, chat up her wicked stepmother Leah? Or, even worse, seek advice from her so-called "real" mother Irene? Beg either woman for advice about how to handle childbirth? Never.

How about getting chummy with her mother-in-law, Gisela? As if that foolish peasant woman would start serving up childbirth tips like hints from Heloise! Now that would be a weird fantasy, enjoying a motherly chat with the short-and-ugly German farm wife, who still hadn't managed to learn decent English. Never had and probably never would.

Oh, such pain!

Neither of Sue's sisters has given birth yet, nor any of her friends and, anyway, she wasn't even supposed to have this baby for another two months. No wonder this 24-year-old doesn't feel ready, plus she's suffering extra because it's all so unfair and not supposed to be happening this soon, and nobody gave her any idea how much it would hurt, not really.

Isn't anybody around here going to help me?

Floating above, I do wish I could help. It's some consolation to know that, in the future, I'll be given many chances to help this mother, to help her year after year after year. All signed up for, not that I remember many details of my Life Contract, since most of those details have pretty much faded by now. (This is standard for a birth.) Most likely, soon I'll forget everything about my heave nly connection, just as this latest mother of mine did when she grew up.

Groaning, this latest mother does bring a certain athletic confidence to her ordeal, writhing and sweating and sending out the terrified animal stink of a woman in labor. *Make it stop*, she's thinking now, in rhythm with her contractions. Because they're coming faster and harder than ever.

Proud to say, Sue just *thinks* her screams. At least she isn't yelling out loud. The same can't be said for the other three women lying on beds in the same delivery room. Second after Sue comes a blonde with long hair, who starts to punctuate her contractions by screaming, "Mommy!"

Then the second woman in labor copies her. Soon the fourth woman in the room joins in. "Mommy! Mommy!" all three are hollering. Hearing this, Sue contracts in a way that has nothing at all to do with back labor.

Mommy! The story of my life. Calling for her ever since I was a kid. But she's not here. Never here. Never coming. Ever.

Once again, Sue recalls her tragic childhood. Between contractions, she seeks consolation through a familiar anguish, both her oldest memory and her most cherished pain.

"Mommy! Mommy! Mommy!" groans the biggest loudmouth again, the one who never shuts up. Sue screams also by now, except that her yelling is still done only inside her head.

That's right, girls. Rub it in.

Sweet sarcasm is Sue's best defense. And, brave soul, doesn't she need that?

Only now I must stop paying attention to her. My time has come, too. Hovering mid-air in my light body, I concentrate on the vortex of light all around me, a light that spirals downward, twirling ever faster, powerful as the pull of a magnet on a stray piece of metal. Soon it feels as though my body of light is being sucked into a tiny tornado funnel; an irresistible force pulling me downward to merge with the baby's body, a merge that's required so that my physical birth can take place.

How I wish that I could delay this merging. Do I really want to deal with this nuisance of a new human body? But Sue is starting to push now, so I find myself pushing, too. Only my version means pushing downward *vibrationally*, that's the main thing — until my energy body merges into that kicking, squirming, terrified, fierce, human body.

Yes, I'm born. Suddenly I'm this baby, forced outside my mother's body, dumped into the room, held by an icy-fingered doctor; all of this happening so unexpectedly, until all I can notice is how I'm breathing air with daggers in it, and I'm feeling so alone. *Earth alone.*

Once born into that delivery room, never do I touch my mother once, nor does she reach out for me. Admittedly, I had been looking forward to some corny kind of birth scene, taking my first physical glimpse of my Mommy, using consciousness to peek out through my closed eyes, and letting my face touch her soft skin and feel her breast ready to feed me.

While growing my body-in-the-womb, I only got to view this mother indirectly, never making direct human contact. Now, as a newborn, I should be able to touch her. How will that feel? Surely this will be different from what I'm used to, stealing pregnancy peeks. (While still inside my mother's body, it was exciting for me when she would look in a mirror. Independently, *I'd look out* through this woman's eyes. Best of all was when I could see my mother's reflection in a full-length mirror.

I wonder, what will change now that I've been born physically? One more human lifetime begun, what will be different from now on, compared to my experiences in the womb?

Crying loudly is my way of asking in human language. Plus, I'm yelling in terror, and why not? My life has begun with an extra reason for screaming: I'm a preemie, born two months too early. At this New York hospital in 1948, that means I'm in mortal danger.

Emergency help is the doctor's priority. Soon as possible, all three pounds, seven ounces — every bit of my red, writhing body — is shoved into a box. It's a place just for me, a place that can save my life, this glass rectangle called an *incubator*.

Laura Sue Rosenbaum, that's the name on my birth certificate. This girl has quite a job now, to lie on her back in that early-model contraption; to lie there alone for the next six weeks; protected from germs and, whenever possible, untouched by human hands.

Incubator technology is still quite new. Many of us premature babies will go blind or even die. Not until many years later will neonatal staff come to understand, cuddling a baby might help her to thrive. She might also find it easier to connect well with other humans.

Eventually, knowledge like this does arrive, but far too late to help me. And speaking of human affection, it will be several long days before my mother or father will be allowed to touch any part of my body. Or even look at me, actually.

In total, three days pass before my parents are permitted even the sight of me, and then they're peering anxiously through a thick glass window at the hospital ward. Squinting, they try to see their sick little girl. She may live or may not. Meanwhile, doctors are doing their best, keeping her safe in a small glass box.

CHAPTER 2

Who Are My People?

Questing Reader, I won't ask you to wait along with me for six weeks in that neonatal ward. Just about anything would be more fun and, fortunately, what I have in mind for you in this chapter will be a lot more interesting. You see, before resuming my story, I'd like to introduce you to the family into which I've been born.

For starters, meet my mother Sue's father, Julius Sussman. Lithuanian-born, his family fled the notorious Pale of Settlement (to get a whiff of the place, think *Fiddler on the Roof*).

Jews who managed to survive the pogroms couldn't escape the poverty, and the number of deaths was astounding; yet somehow the Sussman family arrived in America, and then somehow Julius got himself admitted to Columbia University — quite an achievement, given the school's quota system to help correct The Jewish Problem. Then thanks to another unlikely somehow, this fiercely ambitious immigrant managed to graduate from that Ivy League college. Afterward he pushed his way into business success. Fittingly, in steel.

Before the market crash of 1929, Julius made his family rich. In today's dollars, his net worth would have been at least $14 million. Of course, the tycoon lost it all in the Great Depression, yet he managed to make another million; then finally went broke for keeps.

During my entire childhood, he visited four times, seeming to me like an important man but never a family man. And when he died in a city hospital, all my grandfather's personal effects fit inside a paper bag. In sum, he bequeathed a pair of false teeth plus the last book he ever read, Charles Steinbeck's *Travels with Charlie.*

My mother talked about that as a sad thing. Yet, at the time, I was in high school. Knowing more about Steinbeck than I did about Julius, my take on this paper bag legacy was simply to be impressed at my grandfather's literary taste.

Back while Julius was a fresh Columbia grad and all-around hot prospect, he was beguiled by beautiful Irene, with her perfect blonde hair, enormous blue eyes, and seductive figure. Accomplished, too, Irene could sight-read songs from sheet music, accompanying her pretty voice on the piano.

After being chosen by the eligible bachelor, Irene bore him three demanding daughters: Carol, age 5; my mother Sue, age 3; then the last straw, baby Eleanor, just 1 year old.

Why do I freeze-frame these ages? Because that's when Irene pinned a girlish note to her bedroom pillow. "Julius, I no longer love you. I'm leaving to marry another."

Then Irene kept her word.

Incidentally, why do I call those Sussman girls *demanding?* Merely because all young children are demanding. After their mother's sudden departure, sadly, these kids had to learn how to not *appear* demanding.

Accordingly, the Sisters Three began one of life's harshest jobs, trying their best to wring love out of other people the way you might stand over a kitchen sink, twisting and re-twisting a damp rag to squeeze out any remaining drops of water.

* * *

In her own way, Irene had also been trying her best to find love. Fortunately, modern women now had the vote, flappers could bob their hair and aspire to romantic marriages, and even divorce was becoming fashionable. By 1927, America led the world in divorces. Consequently, scandal stopped being a major deterrent. Experts even conceded that pursuing a divorce didn't *necessarily* debase a woman; and evidently that was all the encouragement needed by independent Irene, who adhered throughout life to her own distinctive set of morals. Whereas other women had affairs with men, she believed in marrying them.

Busily pursuing romantic adventures, Irene didn't really enter my life until I was in high school. By 1962, she had returned to New York, where she married Husband #5, Leon Copland, a Lithuanian Jew like her Husband #1, Julius.

"Nana," as she asked us to call her, began inviting us Rosenbaums to her apartment every Mother's Day. Altogether we went four years in a row. Most vividly, I remember the cocktail franks, a miniature kind of hot dog that I'd never tasted before, cocktail franks which Nana always cooked to crispy perfection. Quite the remarkable food discovery. Every visit, this was my personal highlight.

What else could be expected every visit? Before we left home, Mom would grumble, complaining bitterly that Irene was going to give her an apron.

This prediction always came true. Nana would gush with tone-deaf enthusiasm while bestowing upon my mother a lovely new apron; a present that Sue understandably loathed, since she never, ever wore aprons of any kind, let alone the frilly little numbers favored by ever-flirtatious Irene. Embarrassingly, at sixty, she still wore shorts. And looked good in them.

What else happened during those incredibly slow-moving Mother's Day visits? The old folks — Nana and Leon — were joined by my family of four, plus one other elderly man, Leon's brother Aaron.

This relative always seemed shy and a little out of it, even for a grownup. (To my teenage eyes, old people were perpetually missing the point of... everything). My private explanation was informed by simple New York gaydar. Clearly this man was a homosexual, which must be what made Nana and Leon so uncomfortable. Decades later, I floated my theory by Mom. She laughed uproariously.

"Are you kidding? Your Dad and I were awed by him. As for Irene and Leon, I guess they felt they had to invite him, but neither one was the least bit close to him.

"Besides, I've got to tell you, Irene may have been the most naive woman who ever lived. She kept trying to set Aaron up with women to date, telling me, 'He'd make such a great husband. Just look at how generous he is, like how he lets all those men who are music students live in his house. For free!'"

After the first of these Mother's Day visits, while the four of us drove home in our car, Dad told me that Leon's brother was THE Aaron Copland, one of the greatest composers in American history. Still, the fact of his fame never quite registered on me, not until Lincoln Center opened and then my quiet relative mailed us tickets to hear him conduct *Connotations* in a premiere performance at the new Lincoln Center Philharmonic Hall. We loved it, the Rosenbaum family. Come to think of it, Nana and Leon didn't attend. Actually, Leon didn't really like music.

Liking to be *strong*, that's what mattered for Leon and Nana and just about everybody on my mom's side of the family. Those Sussmans by marriage, like the Sussmans by birth, forced themselves into becoming strong people — even if they didn't often give themselves credit for that, let alone give credit to each other.

Strong Julius became an American success story, with proof in the form of a mansion and factories and daughters three. Differently strong, Irene lived at a time when even one pleasure-seeking divorce could bring social disgrace; yet somehow, she achieved five marriages, including the one to Leon who'd outlive her.

Nana also had one experience of widowhood, courtesy of Hal, Irene's Husband #4. Lung cancer sickened him for years. Even I, who barely met the man, can still hear his horrible cough, as close to a haunting as I've ever witnessed.

* * *

Strong, but so differently strong, were my father's people, the Rosenbaums. Ernie's parents, Hugo and Gisela (GEE-zeh-lah), were a solid couple, coming of age in Hoernsheim, near Frankfurt, Germany; about 40 miles north geographically and, seemingly, 400 years back in time. Gisela worked the family farm while fiancé Hugo apprenticed as a tailor.

Although he was notably spry as a gymnast, there was no money in that kind of work. So, Hugo completed his tailor's apprenticeship, sewing an official masterpiece, then becoming a member of the Tailor's Guild; afterward, never straying from his profession. Except, of course, during World War I when, as a good German, he took a break from tailoring to fight for his Kaiser, winding up as a prisoner of war, trapped in a Siberian prison for five freezing-cold years.

Such a bad news/good news story! Because eventually, with the Russian Revolution, all the prisons were emptied and, thus, prisoners like my grandpa were set free. According to family lore, Hugo walked his way back to Germany; how I wish he'd shared some of those stories with me. Bound by blood, the Rosenbaums may have been, but conversation during our visits was always awkward, as if German-to-English wasn't the only kind of lost in translation.

Lost in translation, or transition, was my father's baby brother Heinz, who died on the terrible sea voyage, dying in a ship packed with refugees fleeing Hitler's Germany. My father, all of three years old, survived that journey; he also triumphed over an almost impossibly inappropriate given name, Ernst (or Ernest) Rosenbaum. From an early age, he found zero "importance in being Ernest" and instead created an outrageously counter-culture life as "Ernie."

Dad's baby sister, my Aunt Ellen, became an educator, as did others on her side of the family. For instance, her husband Butch Hausknecht, gained top status as a sociology professor; my proud Uncle Butch, who didn't merely earn tenure at Lehman College but became head of his department; thoroughly intellectual Butch, the only person I knew in the 1950s who always wore academic-style blue jeans; ruggedly handsome Butch, his brown-eyed face framed by enormous black glasses; my brainy uncle, even more dignified when, away from family gatherings, he led an altogether different and distinguished life as an academic celebrity called Murray instead of Butch -- a highly regarded author, often published in "Dissent Magazine."

His first article there was *The Politics of the Lie Detector*, penned in response to Joe McCarthy's demand that government employees submit to lie detector tests; while his final wry and witty article, published 58 years later, was *Sex, Viagra, and Taxes.*

The other teacher in my family, Uncle Herb Rosenbaum, technically wasn't really an uncle but more like a distant cousin, originally hailing from a nearby part of Germany. Once in America, he bonded with Butch like a brother. Becoming a legendary professor at Hofstra, Herb elevated the standing of that university's Political Science Department to such a degree that it began hosting American Presidential Debates, starting in 2008.

Family visits between these three households (Herb's, Butch's, and Ernie's) were more frequent during my childhood and diminished with the passing years. Apparently, as a baby, I looked more like Herb than anyone else in the family; however, by the time I was old enough to see him as an adult, that bit of resemblance was long gone.

With his piercing eyes and long, witty mouth, Uncle Herb reminded me of a penny with two very different sides. HEADS looked bright, like newly minted copper -- all charisma and kindliness. But TAILS looked more like a worn-out coin, dull and dented and dinged. Secretly, Herb would never forget old hatreds and resentments; deep down he relived Nazi-led horrors that he had witnessed back in the old country. In a doomed attempt to impress him as an adult, I tried bragging to him that one of my books had become a national bestseller in Germany. Herb's response was to growl, "Those Germans would have killed you if they had a chance. Never forget that."

What's the oddest thing about these two high-achiever relatives from my father's side? How I never learned of their stellar achievements from my own parents. Not until researching this part of my memoir did I learn anything about Uncle Butch's writing for *Dissent*, or how Uncle Herb became a Professor Emeritus.

I'm guessing these proud academics must have cruelly disrespected my father. Otherwise, he would have stood first in line to admire their achievements; Ernie was one of the greatest appreciators I've ever known.

Which related detail do I know for a fact? When Uncle Herb, at 80-something, became my Facebook friend, at first I admired him for learning that technology at his advanced age. But eventually I had to unfriend him. Herb persisted in mocking me and my work; among thousands of FB friends that I've had over the years, nobody else has ever treated me thus. But leave it to members of your own human clan to cause the most stinging human pain.

* * *

Ironically, in my own (non-establishment) way, I became a writer and teacher very much like these other relatives on my father's side of the family, although no words of praise for that has ever been uttered by a single one of them. Among all the teachers in my family, my father's younger sister was the one whose work I admired most.

Only an elementary school teacher, my Aunt Ellen insisted on working at a public school in Harlem. Over a career that spanned decades, her caring work was lavished upon kids who would brag to each other, "The rats in my apartment are bigger than the ones in yours."

Unsolved mysteries can be found in every family. About mine I wonder most, why did such an awkwardness develop between my parents and all these other Rosenbaums? Maybe most conversations took place away from my child's ears; even sadder, maybe they never took place at all but, instead, in the manner of continental drift, these brainy and uncommonly caring kinfolk with so much in common… politely inched away from each other's lives, their eyes avoiding each other's eyes, and their noses wrinkling in mutual disdain.

* * *

From my childhood on, Hugo and Gisela Rosenbaum were the relatives I saw most often, especially after my parents moved from Manhattan to Queens; mostly our visits occurred twice a year, very different visits from those awkward ritual celebrations of motherhood with Nana and company.

By contrast, I felt totally comfortable in Grandma Gisela's apartment, third floor up in a solid building with huge cement steps framing the entrance; a dignified old building on the Upper West Side -- soon as you entered, you'd feel at home instantly. It always seemed magical to me, how once the front door of the apartment opened, you'd walk down a long hallway and there you would be. There you'd be, in Germany. Somehow that sequence of steps would transport me back to the Germany of ancient days, maybe because that's how these transplanted relatives inwardly lived still.

Actually, this apartment would have been memorable for the smells alone, mysterious Old World fragrances; fragrances accumulating ever since Hugo and Gisela moved in 1927 to their first (and only) home in America. By the time I made my last family visit there, it was 1964; and I was a high school sophisticate, pretty sure that I knew almost everything of importance about life. Yet in retrospect it's embarrassingly obvious, how much did I really know about my grandparents? Almost exactly nothing.

Grudgingly, for those visits I would put on good clothes and good manners, silently resenting the loss of one of my precious school-free weekend days. While unknowingly, I missed the point of both these honorable people — only decades later would I learn just how honorable.

By my teenage years, Grandma and Grandpa seemed so ancient as to barely be human. At the mere thought of having to join them for another family visit, my bowels would seize up with violently uncomfortable constipation, this happening only when I had to make that semi-annual duty call.

Whatever my age, all family visits were centered in Hugo's living room. Tall and lean, stern to adults but always kindly toward my sister and me, Grandpa was the undisputed head of the family, sitting on the one padded armchair; sitting so proudly erect, his posture couldn't have been any stiffer had he sat on a throne.

All the rest of us plopped down on lesser chairs or else we'd sink into the sofa. This drab-colored, unremarkable-looking sofa had one soft cushion as the sole luxurious touch, a cushion made of shiny satin that was colored silvery gray. Both soft on the eye and glowy to the touch, this was a cushion unlike any I have ever known, and soft in a uniquely pliable way. According to Mom, the softness came from being stuffed with feathers. All I knew was how, however you touched it, that pillow would respond to you, sometimes yielding, other times fluffing itself up from the inside; almost purring, like a cat that really liked you.

Grandma had made that pillow, using feathers from an animal that she had raised and slaughtered. Maybe it was *her* masterpiece, along with Ernie and his sister Ellen, and her grandchildren. But Gisela's girlish days of making adorable, plush pillows were over. Now she sat meekly in the audience as Hugo presided over all conversation. Always he had just one question for me, "What are you learning in school?" By contrast, Grandma Gisela didn't talk to the group at all. She meekly served us meals. However, when I was young, I did spend time together with her, one on one.

Mom told me just one story about these outings with my Grandma, an incident that happened when I was three. Back then, Gisela would babysit me quite often, since my parents'

apartment was nearby. Typically, she would take me to a park
by the Hudson River. On one such occasion, Grandma returned
me to my mother, beaming with happiness, saying, "We had
such a good time. We stopped and looked at the hotsies."

"What?" my mother said. "Hotsies? What are hotsies?"

In her heavily accented English, Gisela described how she had
played with me in the grass, where I discovered some small
purple flowers from clover. "You know," Gisela concluded.
"Hotsies."

Once Sue got the picture she corrected her foolish mother-in-
law. "Mom, in English we call them flowers, not hotsies. Where
did you get that word, anyway?"

"From her," Gisela said. "I figured she knew English better."

"That's your Grandma," Sue would conclude whenever
repeating this story, secure in the knowledge that however bad
she might feel about herself, never would she be quite so
ridiculous as Gisela, taking language lessons from a three-year
old.

* * *

Yes, for years to come, Mom would repeat this story,
triumphant. Meanwhile, as a listener, I had a secret. Because
every repetition of that family lore only intensified a feeling that
I treasured within me, how Grandma understood me better than
my own mother did. Why? Because Gisela and I shared a sense
of wonder, habitually seeking the joy hidden within everyday
things.

When I was age three, who bought my favorite toy? Grandma
Gisela. Every visit I'd grab this treasure just as soon as I could,
my special book, a book just for children, a *Little Golden Book*
with colorful pictures that showed a circus.

One illustration, especially, thrilled me again and again. It pictured how a brightly-colored car contained clowns, colorful clowns in endless supply; clowns that capered out of that small circus car; more and more clowns emerging in an endless supply that was impossible and yet it still happened — because you could see it, right on the page.

Somehow every single one of these clowns fit comfortably into their tiny car; which appeared to me like the kind of miracle I always expected to find all around me, yet seldom did. How the sight of those clowns delighted me! Wonder made that storybook car seem more real to me than all the honking, speeding, shiny cars in all of New York.

You see, Questing Reader, whenever I saw that picture, it reminded me of infinity tucked into this world; not that I possessed such a word as *infinity*. Nor could I summon even a smidgeon of infinity on demand. Sometimes a taste of That would be given me, though. And then, recognizing That, I'd stop whatever else I had been doing at the time.

Of course, I loved that circus book. Unfailingly it delivered a dependable Helloooooooooooooooo from That. Every visit, I'd open up my Golden Book and find my car page. Every time, I could find that mystery, see it on demand, and lose myself in the wonder of it.

As a toddler, I was a thin little girl who didn't much like food, and yet I hungered for that picture, like any crumb I could find of my *real* world, sacred and infinite.

This circus picture reminded me of my real home, a place of Spiritual Truth. Seeing those clowns showed me a hidden world that could open up within this world, a heaven packed with even more wonder than a car stuffed with clowns; a world where I just might find more of what I missed so badly, despite having no words for it yet, neither made-up words like hotsie, nor any of the other words that I heard grownups speak.

Grandma understood that something, I felt. Although I've never spoken of it before, either to her or to anyone else, not until now. It's a story I've saved for you, Questing Reader.

And now that you're all caught up, we can continue together, sharing present-time discoveries in the life of a New York girl named "Laura Sue Rosenbaum."

Let's move forward to a stage when I can do a great many big girl things, all the while clumsily seeking Spiritual Truth.

CHAPTER 3

The Dish and the Spoon

Today I am five years old. This new birthday is going to give me a very good kind of surprise. Mommy and Daddy have explained it to me a lot.

"Preparing me" is what I hear them call it one night, when I'm supposed to be asleep. (For me, of course, what does bedtime mean? The start of that day's most delicious listening, through my open bedroom door.) By now I need to listen more than ever. Since the birth of my baby sister, Amy, listening in secret, I discover the truth. She isn't really just "Getting ready at the hospital, so it can be nice for you when she comes home."

Nope. My parents are scared about having another preemie, and this one even smaller than I was, just 2 pounds, 4 ounces. "Not even the size of a good chicken you'd buy at the store."

It's weird how every night I hear the same thing. Worried voices, and yet they keep telling each other how it couldn't possibly be as bad with Amy as it was with me. Listening, I hear Daddy tell Mommy, "Remember how scared you were that Laura would never be normal?"

News to me! They never told me anything like that, about me not being normal.

Following that part of their ritual, Daddy would tell my mother the rest of his story, the same story every night. Really, just like me, asking to hear my favorite story at bedtime, *The Little Engine that Could.* Until Amy comes home from the hospital, every single night, the rest of Daddy's story goes like this. "Sue, those doctors knew what they were doing with Laura. It's going to be just the same with Amy. So relax. Let's not make ourselves any more neurotic by worrying."

And then he says, "Wait, wait, I've got to go change the record."

That's my Daddy. His favorite toy is our record player. After he comes home from work and hugs Mommy and me, he always starts playing his records; music all day long, until he falls asleep, still listening to music; listening to every kind of music, and it's always so beautiful.

Daddy listens to music on the new Long Playing records, 33 1/3 rpm. He's replacing all the old-fashioned 78s that cram our living room bookcase, 78s from floor to ceiling when I was born. I love that.

Daddy plays music for every mood, but sometimes the mood in the music is not what he feels: like after he talks about the new baby, sometimes he plays ballet music, which is a happy kind of record, quick little stories made of music, stories that have no words. This music, sounding like candy, is Mommy's favorite.

By the day I turn five, Amy has come home from the hospital and lived with us for a very long, long time. Months! Mostly I understand her okay. One of the most annoying things about her, actually, is how Amy still speaks perfect Telepathy. Mine hardly works anymore. Sometimes, though, I can feel it: talking to me in that sweet baby way, with her bright bunches of ideas like dandelion bouquets. She'll throw those bunches of ideas at me and everybody else, which annoys me like crazy.

For now, I can still make myself catch them, only I'm too big to pick up Telepathy bursts on my own and fling them myself; and I miss that terribly, how I used to pick up my own shiny bunches of words made of energy.

Why is Telepathy going away? I don't understand. Did my parents make that happen, since I'm supposed to be a big girl now? Me, a big sister, which — if anyone asked, I could have told them — told them in human words too —— "I never asked for that."

Being a big sister? My parents keep telling me that Big Sister is supposed to be so great. If they asked, here's exactly what I would tell them: "No." Of course, I would remember to use my manners and say, "Please, no. No and thank you." But somehow this mostly awful thing of having to become a big sister happened anyway.

I do like Amy, at least some of the time, although she receives far too much attention from people, as if she were the only adorable person in the family now; also, she needs so much help because of being a baby and weakish, like how I used to be.

It makes me happy to comfort her, since Mommy and Daddy can't do that part so well. For one thing, they don't know how scary it is for her, which I can understand perfectly. So, I'll tell her how my body became perfectly normal, just like hers will, too. This calms her right down and takes away that extra-scowly face she makes when she's crying hard from being terrified that she might never be normal.

For another thing, I can help Amy understand some of the ugly things about our life, like the cigarette smoke everywhere. When I lived inside Mommy, I saw her always smoking a cigarette. She told a friend proudly, "Ernie and I are both chain smokers, 3 ½ packs a day. If that cigarette isn't in my mouth, it's burning on an ashtray where I can reach for it immediately."

Seemed to me, even back when I lived inside my mother, while she explained her love of cigarettes somehow she was bragging; boasting in a clever way without using words, like telling her friend, "Smoking so much makes us extra-sophisticated." So far,

I don't know what sophisticated is. But she and Daddy sure are desperate to have it.

Long ago, when I came home from the hospital and started to live in the apartment, the smelly air gave me a choking feeling all the time. Sometimes, I felt scared to breathe, like there were monsters; and the only thing that helped was going outside in my stroller for Mommy's sanity walks. Eventually I figured it out. Cigarettes aren't just something that you put in your mouth and puff and make ash pieces with and then you play cute with putting the ash pieces into the ashtray.

Cigarettes make the air thick and dirty and stinky. But in the language of energy, what tobacco does is even worse. The sweet, heavy energy from cigarettes makes earth energy stronger but chases away the heavenly energy from Home. So every night, I explain things like this to my little sister.

Amy is very curious. Teaching her comes easily to me, and I discover things while I'm teaching, like when I explain to her about the cigarettes, or how not to be scared when we hear Mommy crying every day during our nap time. I explain that when we grow up, we will not have to be sad, and we won't have to be like our mother in other ways, either; hiding feelings so much and always worrying her secret worry about going crazy. By now, I have been in the world quite a lot, so I know, not everybody worries as much as our Mommy. Teaching Amy, while we're alone together in our special nursery bedroom — it's one of my very favorite things.

The walls here are a pretty shade of light blue. Hung on the walls are special pictures, made of a thick kind of cardboard, three colorful pictures with special shapes. Daddy has explained to me how these special pictures are supposed to make children happy, because they come from a nursery rhyme that all children learn.

Hey, diddle, diddle,

The cat and the fiddle,

The cow jumped over the moon.

The little dog laughed to see such sport,

And the dish ran away with the spoon.

Since I have memorized that rhyme by now, I can understand in a big girl way what hangs on the wall of my bedroom.

> ➢ One picture shows a cow. Black and white and friendly, with big eyes.

> ➢ Another picture is shaped like the moon, a crescent moon, like a big smile, only instead of going sideways like a regular smile, this moon stands up-and-down, as if getting ready to walk.

> ➢ The third colorful shape on the wall shows a dish and a spoon. They have hands, and are holding hands to show love to each other, always. Just like Amy and I are supposed to do.

Cute little baby Amy, Grrrrr! She can speak Telepathy perfectly, while I can hardly do it anymore, which makes me so frustrated I want to cry; especially when Amy smiles at me in that bragging way babies sometimes do secretly in front of their big sister, something they never do in front of a grownup because they're so good at acting like their only face is innocent and adorable.

Oh, that smug look! Just because she still can speak Telepathy better than me — well, that is only one of Amy's many ways to be so, so annoying. Another way is how she grabs way too much attention from Mommy and Daddy. And for what? Just for being a baby? It's not fair.

According to Mommy, I have been saying that a lot lately, "It's not fair."

Well, it isn't. Also, as a big four-year-old, I have found one special doll, the only doll I like; he's a little boy made of thick rubber, and very colorful, with a shirt and pants painted on, bright yellow hair and big blue eyes and red lips. He smells great, unlike any other doll. His name is Terry (wherever I found that name, nobody knows) and I talk to him a lot, especially when things aren't fair.

Unfair! Like what happened on my one special treat, so far, as the big girl in the family. For a special treat, I got to have a sleepover with Grandma and Grandpa, staying overnight in Grandpa's special tailor room, with his treadle sewing machine in one corner and, to the right, there were tin containers filled with thread, round spools of thread in every color you can imagine, bright threads on perfectly round spools. Over to the other side was the big bed where I got to sleep, with a pretty flowered coverlet that must have come with them from Germany.

Except that what happened while I slept... wasn't pretty. All night long, nightmares kept coming. Scariest of all, on waking, my eyes were glued shut, stuck right onto my face. Really, I couldn't open my eyes the least bit; it was like suddenly going blind. So, I hollered and cried as loud as I could, and then I screamed even louder, until finally Grandma came.

I could hear her run into the room and then she spoke in a quiet voice, a steady kind of voice that I didn't know my grandmother had. Talking to me she used a voice that felt so gentle and kind, just like the touch of her hands; soft hands that somehow knew a way to comfort me until I hardly needed to cry anymore; and then with her wise, old hands Grandma placed a special cloth over my eyes, a washcloth that she made just warm enough with water from the sink.

And for a very long time, she used that special healing cloth; using it even after my last little squirts of tears stopped. Grandma kept putting that fresh, warm cloth over my eyelids until all the sticky crusts came off and I could open my eyes again. Finally, I could see.

"You just got a cold in your eye," Grandma told me, explaining so I wouldn't be scared about what happened. She even showed me the little crusts on her white washcloth; just some silly yellow crusts that couldn't hurt me anymore ever again.

I looked at her then, my funny old Grandma, with her very small brown eyes and the short, bristly, steel-gray eyebrows that matched her hair; no hairstyle for her but just a bunch of steely old hair, like a mop on her head; and I took a good look at her short, wide nose, such a good match with her short, thin mouth; mostly, though, what I saw and loved was a lot of soft skin on her cheeks.

She was so full of wrinkles, and just then with my eyes able to see once again, how did that face of hers look? So kind and very beautiful.

Later, back home, I thought about that special time with Grandma. I felt like it taught me something, and eventually I figured out what. Even adventures like a bad sleepover can turn out well by the end.

That's good to know because today I'm going to have my biggest adventure yet, even bigger than a sleepover. On this birthday, when turning five, what is my present going to be? For the first time since becoming a big sister, I will get to be important in the family again. (Very, very fair, by the way.)

I am going to have the special treat called *an operation*. My parents have explained to me what will happen at the hospital, my special birthday present for turning five. Also, how it's going to make me the opposite of sick.

Questing Reader, I'm pretty embarrassed to tell you this. Last year I had to drop out of preschool. Getting sick was the reason. Nobody in the family liked how I'd go to school one day, catch a new cold from some other kid, and then stay sick in bed for a week. Once I was healthy enough to go back, it would start all over again, driving Mommy crazy.

If anybody asked, I could tell them that I don't like that sick kind of life, either. Because it always goes like this. Bringing me meals in bed, Sue puts on her big, brave smile like, "I am a perfect mother. And you are so lucky to have me. Because I never had a good mother but instead my father Julius married Leah, the wicked stepmother."

Afterward, while I try to eat my soup, Mommy tells me the story of her tragic childhood. Another bedtime story for grownups, making her feel so happy when she repeats it over and over!

Would somebody please explain this to me? How is her telling that story different from when I suck my thumb? Yes, I still do that although I'm turning five. I do it for comfort, even though grownups call it a terrible, bad, babyish habit.

Meanwhile Mommy tells us certain stories every single day, and that's supposed to be "Something I need to tell you, so that you can be grateful for how lucky you are and how you have everything so easy."

Grownups like to tell ridiculous stories. These make as little sense as a dish holding hands with a spoon and running *anywhere*. Just ridiculous! Like how, I guess, they now prefer my silly little baby sister. And that's all the family I get? You can see why I long for a big brother.

But I do thank my Mommy for doing one really good, smart thing when I kept getting sick, almost as good as getting me a big brother. Finally, she asked the doctor, "Why does Laura keep getting all those colds?"

What did he tell her? The problem was my sick tonsils. So, on this birthday, my parents have found a special doctor who will take those tonsils away forever, pull them right out of my body.

When the tonsils are gone, I will not get sick anymore. Mommy warns me that I might not like the operation itself, but what will I like very much? All the fun that comes later. For instance, after I wake up with those bad tonsils gone forever, I can eat ice cream, all the ice cream I want, and that's a promise.

So here I am now, lying on a special hospital bed, wearing my regular panties with little flowers on them. But also I'm in a special dress that comes from the hospital, a funny dress made of skinny cloth, and it has strings that tie in back.

Air around here smells awful, like medicine. Still the doctor and nurse are trying hard to be nice and make me comfortable. It's kind of cute, really. They are using those trying-so-hard voices that most grownups have when talking to kids, a fake voice used especially for children.

Their fake voices sound like this: "I am big and smart. You are little and stupid. I will use tiny words and make my face look extra-sweet. That way you can understand all the words that I say. My, but I'm so proud of myself! How good am I at talking to children!"

The problem with people like this is that they have completely forgotten what it's like to be a child. Very few grownups remember. Daddy does sometimes. My Grandma Gisela remembers always.

Lying in my hospital bed, I think about her tiny brown eyes, so full of playing, plus her squishy big nose. Grandma's mouth doesn't smile a lot, especially when other grownups are around. With me, though, a special smile comes out. Whenever it's just the two of us, we are like special friends.

While waiting for my operation, I think about Grandma on purpose. Mostly I promise myself, when I'm grown up, I will do exactly what I'm doing right now. Questing Reader, I'll do my best to have fun *without* waiting for some bad part to happen any minute — which happens to be what Mommy does all the time, although Daddy keeps telling her, "Would you please quit worrying already?"

No, I won't become a grownup who worries. Especially I refuse to worry about this operation. I am going to make my parents proud of me and will not cry.

Into my hospital room comes a tall doctor, who says he is going to put a cloth over my head and then I will fall asleep. Easy as pie! When I wake up, my tonsils will be gone forever.

CHAPTER 4.

Not Just Remembering. Being There

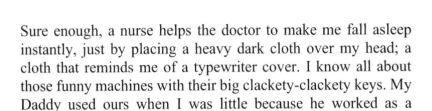

Sure enough, a nurse helps the doctor to make me fall asleep instantly, just by placing a heavy dark cloth over my head; a cloth that reminds me of a typewriter cover. I know all about those funny machines with their big clackety-clackety keys. My Daddy used ours when I was little because he worked as a reporter. At night, he would type his newspaper stories. My parents have told me that's how I became a good little sleeper who didn't mind noise.

Daddy has a different job now, but we still own his typewriter. When not playing with it, you're supposed to cover the keyboard with a thick, slick kind of dress that fits the typewriter just so, a typewriter outfit in a strange material, heavy, like clothing mixed with mud.

Wonderful! Thanks to that funny-smelling cloth from the hospital, I'm moving through space now, moving as if I flew only yesterday, speeding through the air as if I'm used to flying every single day, as if flying has become normal for me again. How absolutely wonderful! I'm back in my body of light, the kind that I wore before coming to earth as Laura.

Oh, God, I remember you now, recognizing a faint smell of you, the smell of *akasha* (big space). I'm starting to feel your presence again, like something very quiet that never really went away.

What happened between us lately, God? Did we have a fight or something? Anyway, it's like we're making up now. In my heart I'm laughing, then hugging that bit of You closer to me, until it feels as if my body remembers the *normal* way to be, no more struggling with the *herky-jerky little girl body* that I've been learning to live in.

Also, it's such a relief to be flying again. I mean, walking is okay. Running and jumping feel good, plus I'm proud that I learned how to skip before I had to leave preschool. But none of that could ever feel as good as what I'm doing now. Nothing ever feels as good as flying.

Flying super-fast, at whatever speed I want, what's next? Quick as anything, I glide through a silvery tunnel, glowing with a faint fairy-ish light of palest blue. Then pop! Out the other side I come. Then I start moving through a really big space, a big-enough place finally, where flying feels even more normal.

My angels are flying along with me, Terry and the other two. (That's interesting, being with these guys again.) We're all smiling and I'm starting to get the most wonderful feeling. Could it be that I am going back to my home world?

I am. I am! Yes, I am.

What happens next? I'm back in my normal body again, which is actually a very big deal, and I've also landed back Home. You see, Questing Reader, my human-type body is okay... except it's constantly jerking my attention backward, interrupting me with ideas like *Careful* and *Ouch* and *Wait, you can't do that yet.*

Now that I'm back in my normal body, all that heckling has stopped, making it possible for me to notice something else, an even bigger deal: all the love. I start to feel how some of the love in this place is just for me; and it's a love-that-helps-you-learn-so-easily, no struggle and no hurt feelings. So familiar is this love that, breathing it in, I feel a bouncy, shining rightness start to flow like a fountain within me. Oh yes, I remember that feeling.

About that normal body of mine, let me describe it to you, Questing Reader, just in case you've forgotten what it's like to have yours. From the outside, I guess I look like a ball of light. Quite different from what kids like me are used to, with mysterious hidden bones that are supposed to be growing, plus places on the outside that you can see what's inside, like skin where you could get cut and need a Band-Aid.

What a relief to be back in my energy body, which feels totally safe, yet also is constantly changing, with edges of pulsating energy that move outward and then dissolve, kind of like the waves at Jones Beach where they're breaking along the shore. Gone are illusions like "I'm a little girl" or "I'm a girl" or "I'm a little." Instead, I'm simply myself, an ancient being. As usual. With my heavenly name, made of music.

Sure does feel good, having my name back! And what else is back. It's my Telepathy, which I used to take for granted until about the time I dropped out of preschool. All that Energy Speak used to be my biggest fun. Here it's back, and as natural as having fingernails... which I don't seem to have any more, hmmm, but who misses that?

Just as delicious as returning to my rightful body and mind, I love the clarity of whatever I feel and see and know. Like waking up from a dull dream, I have regained my ability to be aware at many planes of existence simultaneously. Needless to say, I can stop thinking and talking like a little kid. Once again I can use right-sized language to analyze or discern or imagine whatever I like, no more limits that result from having my thoughts confined to a child's intelligence. Or to human intelligence, either!

Other beings are here. I start feeling them now, so many friends thronging around me, and they're absolutely beaming to see me as well. Instantaneously we recognize each other as if I had never left. Together we create our hum, like a hive of welcoming sounds, back-and-forth between each of us, with an overall harmony of everyone buzzing and learning together... until it feels as though all the joy will never stop.

Soon I will share learning with every single one of my friends, or maybe I already am (in one of my dimensions). However, there's one big conversation that I need to have right now. With God. Yes, now that I'm adjusted to my angel body, we can talk together properly.

Suddenly, quick as that thought, we are.

OF COURSE, I LOVE YOU.

God gets to the point right away, wrapping me around in His no-body body. And I love how He's so strongly in everything, twinkling away, like dimples on a human face that smiles.

He-She is humming through space, through colors, through everything. Nonetheless, being everywhere doesn't make God hard to find. Opposite that. I can taste That Presence easily, like finding the flavor in a big glass of my favorite drink back in the big city apartment, sipping a very grown-up treat called *chocolate milk.*

God is saying:

OF COURSE, I STILL LOVE YOU. EVERY SAD FEELING, EVERY TEAR. DID I HEAR IT? MORE THAN HEAR IT, I FELT IT. LOOK INTO MY FACE OF EVERYWHERE. CAN YOU DOUBT THAT I'VE BEEN WITH YOU EVERY SECOND?

If I weren't shaking so hard, mixed with joy, I would be saying, "But, but, but."

However, God answers my questions without me having to ask them.

FIRST, LET'S clear UP WHAT HAPPENED WHEN YOU WERE IN THE WOMB. I KNOW YOU HAD SECOND THOUGHTS. YOU CALLED FOR A MISCARRIAGE.

NOW THAT YOU'RE BACK HERE, LET'S REMEMBER THE RULE ABOUT THAT. WHILE YOU'RE PREPARING A NEW HUMAN BODY, DURING WOMB TIME, A SOUL IS ALWAYS ALLOWED TO CHANGE YOUR MIND AND SAY "STOP." AFTERWARD YOU CAN RETURN HOME, NO WORRIES.

EXCEPT THAT, IN YOUR CASE, FOR THIS PARTICULAR LIFETIME, I SAID NO. DEFINITELY I HEARD YOU ASKING. AND ASKING MORE THAN ONCE. YET STILL I SAID NO.

PROBABLY THE WORST PART WAS THAT YOU'VE HAD TO WAIT FOR ME TO EXPLAIN WHY. MAYBE YOU'RE WONDERING, WHY DIDN'T I EVER, EVEN ONCE, EXPLAIN WHY? NOT EVEN GIVE YOU THE SATISFACTION OF A DIRECT ANSWER. WHY DID I SILENTLY TELL YOU "NO," LEAVING NO CLUES?

Grrrr, worst part indeed! In response, I show God a shuffle view of my most miserable faces from womb time, and then all those days alone in the incubator. Sad faces, hopeless faces, angry faces, terrified faces. Then I repeat this sequence again about a zillion more times, until I feel satisfied that I've made my point.

DID YOU HAVE THE RIGHT TO ASK FOR A MISCARRIAGE? ABSOLUTELY. ESPECIALLY BECAUSE YOU BEGAN TO REALIZE WHAT A TOUGH ASSIGNMENT YOU HAD CHOSEN.

At which point I strongly agree. Then I want to sum up why I didn't — and still don't — want to go through with that terrifying incarnation.

In orderly fashion, God instantly sorts through my outburst, sending the different components right back to me, all the main points returning to me like a sympathetic sort of echo.

1. It got to me just as soon as I became physically bound to Sue's body.

2. Feeling all her pain and seeing others through her eyes? So ugly!

3. Every week it got worse, adjusting to the misery, hers and the family's.

4. At this time in history, all humans were recovering from earth's most hideous war ever. That sure didn't help.

5. Very soon, my planned incarnation for the foreseeable future — wham! It hit me like being smacked in the face.

6. I'm no coward.

7. But I know my limits. So I said, "No, I can't do this. Make it stop."

8. God, you could easily have fixed that for me. Only you didn't.

9. And I asked so many times before giving up. So. Many. Times.

10. Never did I imagine You would ever ignore me like that. Did You hate me or what?

God continues:

LET ME TELL YOU WHY IT HAPPENED THAT WAY, WHY YOUR REQUEST WAS DENIED, NOT ONLY THE FIRST TIME BUT EVERY OTHER TIME THAT YOU ASKED.

ALL THIS MADE YOU FEEL SO BAD ABOUT YOURSELF. I DON'T WANT YOU TO FEEL BAD ABOUT YOURSELF, NOT EVER. FEEL ME HOLDING YOU NOW, FEEL THAT LOVE, AND THEN I'LL KEEP ON EXPLAINING.

CAN YOU REMEMBER HOW YOU PREPARED FOR THAT LIFE? WHEN YOU MADE YOUR LIFE CONTRACT, YOU WERE REMINDED OF ALL THOSE ILLUSIONS AND WHY THEY WOULD BE NECESSARY. IN DETAIL, YOU WERE WARNED ABOUT YOUR FAMILY SITUATION. THEREFORE, BY THE TIME YOU AGREED TO THAT CONTRACT, YOU KNEW EXACTLY WHAT YOU WERE GETTING INTO. AND WHY.

BOTH YOU AND I KNOW HOW MUCH COURAGE IT ALWAYS TAKES TO INCARNATE ON EARTH. A SOUL MUST BE SO BRAVE EVERY TIME, REGARDLESS OF HOW MANY TIMES YOU'VE DONE IT BEFORE.

AND YES, YOU'RE RIGHT. USUALLY, A SOUL DOES HAVE THAT DISCRETION DURING WOMB-TIME, THE RIGHT TO REQUEST A RETURN TRIP. AN AUTOMATIC APPROVAL, NO QUESTIONS ASKED, WHICH IS HOW MOST MISCARRIAGES HAPPEN. ONLY I DO RESERVE THE RIGHT TO OVERRIDE SUCH A REQUEST. ALTHOUGH THIS ISN'T WELL KNOWN, STILL, ON RARE OCCASIONS, I WILL DO AN OVERRIDE. WHICH IS EXACTLY IS WHAT HAPPENED WITH YOU.

HOW COME? FIRST OFF, I KNEW — YES, KNEW — THAT YOU COULD HANDLE THIS LIFETIME. GRANTED, YOUR MOTHER'S INCARNATED FORM IS QUITE DAMAGED. ALSO, YOU'D HAVE TO STRUGGLE FOR THE FIRST YEARS JUST TO STAY ALIVE. PARTLY YOU WOULD BE PAYING BACK KARMA BUT MOSTLY YOU VOLUNTEERED BECAUSE... WELL, DON'T YOU REMEMBER?

CHAPTER 5

Planning My Life Contract

In a flash, I'm remembering it heaven-style, my Planning Meeting for the Laura lifetime. Only the memory is broadcasting in real-time-me-time, a memory show like the TV shows that I used to love back in New York.

Quick as having Mommy turn on *Howdy Doody*, I'm back in a golden room with an easy-to-recognize background hum. This announces, Planning Meeting for a New Lifetime at Earth School, accompanied by an excited, accomplishing joy, like a bee near some exceptionally tasty flowers.

To set the scene in your imagination, Questing Reader, be sure to include a stately shade of rose gold in the air, the kind reserved for something sacred even by heavenly standards, a Divinely-blessed ceremony of life planning. Start to imagine all that and soon you'll be hovering right along with me.

Who's in charge? A Divine Being, ancient as a glacier, with an uncanny knowing that can flash like lightning. He's a soul that can move in consciousness through any person, lighting up layer after layer of pure truth. Around here, that's known as being an Ascended Master. This one's name is Merlin.

And what does he call me? *YOU.* Given how he thinks it, that's name enough, and it plucks a sort of joy within me as if he were playing a harp. Quite typical for any meeting like this, thousands of beings attend. Makes sense. Often. I've come to other people's Planning Meetings: Sometimes to cheer on friends;

other times to encourage a complete stranger, sharing in the mystery of incarnation; occasionally just for entertainment, because Planning Meetings are amazing. No circus or concert on earth could compare, since a meeting like this is real-life history in the making. It's a privilege to attend, getting to hum heavenly encouragement, amplifying the wonder.

Planning Meetings might be the greatest art form ever, since what happens is nothing less than this: A soul shapes a new incarnation, then boldly commits. Quite the contrast to Life Reviews, when a soul comes out the other end.

Frankly this returning to heaven to learn about your recent incarnation… it's like coming out the poop end of life… in contrast to the restaurant-like, lip-smacking deliciousness of a Planning Meeting. Around here we have this saying, "Planning Meetings for joy. Life Reviews for… compassion."

Basically, watching a Life Review makes you want to hunker down with some celestial tissues, feeling sorry for the sad parts of the story, consoling yourself with knowledge of growth that took place anyway, and maybe wondering if you'll ever risk leaving heaven again. By contrast, how do you feel after watching an inspiring Planning Meeting? You can't wait to leave.

As for attending my own Planning Meeting, I'm tempted to call the spiritual pleasure *unique and indescribable*. Then I might stop right there, smiling with smug delight. Only that would be a really obnoxious way to treat you, Questing Reader. Instead, I'll wrap some words around the event and attempt to describe things properly. Just don't expect me to fully convey the beating heart of it.

Actually, Questing Reader, by now you might have started to vaguely remember Planning Meetings of your own, ones just like mine, only swapping in different details. Obviously, you couldn't be on earth now, reading these words, unless you'd already scored loads of memories like this one. But if you're not feeling it yet, simply picture a sort of high stakes sporting event attended by thousands. Only this kind of event is spiritual, with participants glowing beneath a spotlight of extra-bright Divine love.

Right from the start, this particular Planning Meeting feels momentous, larger in scope than more recent ones in my long history as a soul. Even the spectators seem to feel it, a sense of portent that brings an almost electrical fizz to the room -- not because I'm so gosh-darned special but due to the approaching time in earth's history, shifting from the Age of Faith to the Age of Awakening.

Everyone here knows big history's coming, and soon. Therefore, thousands of momentous Life Contracts are being made now, contracts that will be very much like mine; and lately I've been to similar Planning Meetings for other souls who, by now, have incarnated on wacky Earth School.

Only I'm sure not feeling, "Same old, same old." Planning Meetings could be compared to wedding ceremonies. No matter how many you've attended, it just might feel a bit different if your role there is… getting married! To start things off, Merlin sends out a telepathic bundle of knowledge, like the start of a fireworks display.

Gathering here, we celebrate earth, which is about to change almost beyond recognition. Around here, we call what's happening The Awakening Project. *Everyone involved in this project will give a direction to changes set in motion long ago. Magnificent changes, and inevitable. Changes whose quality will be influenced by the souls who incarnate next, especially by souls committed to bringing spiritual awakening into earth.*

As all of you know, every world in creation is a spiritual schoolroom, shaped with ingenious creativity, and lit up with astral frequencies.

Earth has always been unusual, though, purposely designed with very, very, low frequencies. Almost unbelievably low, those Astral Vibrational Frequencies!

Just how low? Humans must take on qualities that are entirely different from other incarnational worlds. Hence the technical term so famous throughout the universe, Human Vibrational Frequencies. *Nicknamed* Low and Slow. *Or, even less flattering,* Dumb and Dumber.

All of you here at this Planning Meeting know from past experience, how earth is the toughest of all the learning planets. Inevitably that kind of life changes you forever, even if you dare to humanly incarnate on earth only once. Sacrificing all that you know in your heavenly world, you agree to inhabit a fragile animal body, living in a world brimming with fear, pain, loneliness; greed, anger, and all the other illusions.

How hard is it, adjusting to earth life? Many incarnated adults only appear grown up. *Inwardly they're still protesting like teenagers. These angels in human form never manage to accept earth's harsh and dumbed-down vibrational frequencies, no matter how many years they breathe air and however strongly their human hearts beat.*

Understandably so. Every normal adjustment to human life could be considered a triumph, especially in the waning years of the Age of Faith. Even if nothing else were strange about human lifetimes in this era, growing into adulthood takes decades: learning how to run the body, developing a sense of self, managing money. Then, depending upon the particulars of a Life Contract, additional challenges will add to that lifetime's intense potential for education.

➢ *Can this human game prove rewarding? Possibly.*
➢ *Hard? Inevitably.*

Maybe you're wondering, then, all of you who have gathered here to witness this Planning Meeting... Maybe you're wondering, why bother to incarnate on earth? Why dumb down into a human life form?

Here's my quick answer for you. Vibrationally, humans are the lowest of the low... but caring.

CHAPTER 6.

The Awakening Project

"Whatever," I'm thinking by now. "Tell me already, tell me. What are you offering me this time?"

As if he can read my mind — which of course, he can — Merlin takes a different tack. He says:

To begin, I'll describe what is wholly routine about the new life planned for YOU. Much like your previous earth experiences, YOU will take on a body at those low-slow Human Vibrational Frequencies. Granted, the plan built into this incarnation is for YOU to start adapting a bit slower than most, eventually overcoming those early challenges and becoming normal enough.

Progressing into adult life, YOU will slow down and dumb down. Playing the typical human game, reluctantly but inevitably, what will happen? Most of YOUR intelligence will fall away, except for the collection of talents always built into a human lifetime, consolations to light YOUR way, talents like clues on a treasure map. In practice "talent" means whatever brings YOU joy. Following joy will help YOU to carry out your purpose for that lifetime.

At the delicious thought of having a new set of talents, I blurt out a bit of dazzle, what would look like a smile… if I were human. Many others dazzle up a bit. Questing Reader, I guess that's because anyone who's survived an earth lifetime has gained great respect for the consolation of talent.

Merlin seems to notice that dazzle of joy in our group, since he sends out his next packet of knowledge with, perhaps, a bit of extra bounce.

Will YOU have your share of joy and talent in that incarnation? Definitely.

But will YOU also face the typical struggle to grow up and adjust? Indeed!

Eventually YOU will become an adult, supposedly wiser than children but, really, far duller. Despite that, YOU will have that distinctive feature of most adult human dullards: caring.

A big reaction comes from the crowd. Colorful lights surge through the air, lustrous pink and other pastels, until I feel my own soul start to crave it -- human caring, sweet and surprising every time single time, with a gimme-more quality, just like candy. Merlin chuckles:

Calm down. Let's not go all soft in the head just because some of you still remember that tasty human caring.

One guy in attendance shoots upward a big curling ribbon of thought in the most luscious shades of blue. "Merlin, you've called it delicious, and I remember how addictive it can be. Yet that caring is also sacred, right?"

Merlin responds:

Yes. Human caring can elevate the heavy dullness of earth, giving rise to a unique magnificence. In the Life Contract being planned here, incarnated YOU will never lose that human ability to care, so unique in all the universe.

Why does Earth School attract souls like all of you at this Planning Meeting? Because of one thing. Confusing though that place seems to be, every day of a human lifetime brings potential for exceptionally rapid spiritual growth. Completing any human Life Contract, regardless of how well or badly, a soul will gain wisdom.

What is the worst case? After suffering through a life that feels like a dismal failure, that soul will be rewarded still, marked forever by a distinctive radiance and compassion.

Oh, the suspense! I tell Merlin, "Okay, that part I get. What's going to be different this time?"

A Shift to earth is due to begin on a date long foretold. On December 21, 2012, it will start: Earth's Age of Awakening.

Included in that worldwide transformation, all humans alive will develop a new vibrational freedom, a flexibility to move in consciousness from Human Vibrational Frequencies to Astral Vibrational Frequencies, or vice versa. People will even gain the potential to see at the Divine Vibrational Frequency, and to do this while still engaged in everyday life.

In short, the Shift signals a change in how human consciousness functions. Regarding that new vibrational freedom to position consciousness, this can bring greater wisdom. Humans can do better, inwardly, at making sense of their lives. Ultimately, this consciousness change will be even more momentous than the Ice Age. However, that change will also be subtle, not altering earth's physical reality. As a result, materialistic people may never notice anything different. Thought Leaders will have work to do.

For how long will humans be confused by their subtle, new, inner freedom? That will depend, won't it? For centuries to come, the inner quality of human experience may depend on you, all of you who volunteer for The Awakening Project.

How many of you adventurous souls will choose to incarnate now as humans? A thrilling adventure awaits you. Imagine being able to help bring a positive direction to spiritual awakening for all of posterity. Unquestionably, big changes are inevitable. The best case will be a triumph of spiritual awakening, even Spiritual Enlightenment for many.

But what's the alternative? Humanity may squander this chance to evolve faster spiritually, setting in motion in a dismal future that could last for centuries.

We Divine Beings who are helping to fashion the latest batch of Life Contracts, we know how important it is for strong souls to incarnate now into Earth School. Leaders must be souls who have already attained considerable courage and stubbornness, souls ready to begin their new lifetimes with that advantage. Under your leadership, you can bring to light new ideas about what can become possible in the Age of Awakening.

All of you here are invited to help. Dare to recognize, this is an invitation to glory. Like all who live on earth for the decades that follow the Shift, you can place your personal imprint upon this historic time. Energetically, your own hand will be upon that future, an imprint that can help to shape quality of life for humankind.

Along with that prospect, let's be clear. Bringing honor to this lifetime will require every bit of strength that you've got. And why? You'll be unlike billions of humans who will also be living on earth. They will not actively care about bringing spiritual truth into the world. Unlike them, you can awaken your leadership potential. To help you do that, you will carry within your heart a soul-level version of the spiritual preview being imparted to each of you right now.

Granted, it may be hard for all of you who carry that touchstone of truth. Sadly, even some of you may become soul-blind while living on earth after the Shift. For that reason, I call upon you to swell the ranks of the Awakening Project, personally growing into spiritual awareness until, gradually, the truth can dawn upon you consciously and clearly, how your goal is to help awaken humanity.

Unique patience will be required. Neither will you spread a religious kind of message, nor will you bring understanding through traditional means, like speaking before large assemblies.

Success cannot come in such ways. Waking up consciousness isn't like joining a club. Nor is spiritual discernment accomplished through hero worship. Instead, your most effective leadership will involve gently reminding individual humans that they can trust the truth within themselves. Then you'll encourage them to seek authentic teachers who possess that quintessential human attribute, caring.

Adding to your challenges, as leaders of the Awakening Project, most of you will go incognito. Thus, it may take you many earth years to

*find your fellow leaders, nor can any of you expect to personally
receive vast public fame as a leader.*

*Ironically earth will have become far noisier than at any previous time
you remember, with celebrities braying their nonstop empty noise, and
foolish advice lauded as wisdom, and big* personalities *admired
mainly for being famous, and* successful *attention seekers who
seemingly get away with indulging their basest desires.*

*Accordingly, the truth that you volunteers will aim to spread – it
cannot move through the usual social channels. True spiritual
awakening happens in silence, secluded, in deep privacy. While
integration of spiritual wisdom is earned through one free will choice
at a time, earned by living in integrity, by doing one's reasonable best
even if nobody else is watching.*

*Will the Awakening Project succeed? Not necessarily. Yes, I'm
warning all of you about that. Although I don't really believe in the
lesser outcome. Nonetheless, it's true that earth could go either way.
Hopefully earth will evolve into freedom for most -- and spiritual
liberation, even, for millions.*

*Alternatively, there may be a preponderance of dullness, confusion
and... well... what around here we call* failed experiments. *That's why
I urge everyone here to take Planning Meetings like this one very
seriously. Hear my message as though it's directed personally at you.
I'm calling on every single one of you to recognize this glorious
opportunity and volunteer.*

Merlin leans toward me now. Not as a famed Ascended Master but as
my personal teacher over many lifetimes.

Sure, his thought packets always carry great power, but now they're
like miniature roses, poufing into the air, releasing petals and scent;
and I feel a familiar, craggy tenderness as he asks me, *"Do you think
that you understand well enough what will be happening at the start
of The Age of Awakening?"*

Embarrassed, I emit a kind of gulp to convey, "Not really."

CHAPTER 7.

The Map

Then let me show YOU, Merlin says.

With a simple wave of one hand, Merlin creates a strategic map of earth, a map that hovers in the air, reminding me of the old-fashioned military maps that generals have used during wartime, a map where pushpins would indicate where troops were deployed.

As he speaks next, Merlin's map zooms in, enlarging to show details of the U.S.A. Many black dots, like pushpins, are already in place, hundreds of individual dots spreading across America, not clustered together but each one seemingly placed at random.

Volunteers are being sent to places like these. If you join them, here's what will happen to most of you. Unless uncommonly fortunate, you will be born into a pretty broken family, living in a community that does not support you in the manner of a traditional earth community.

So you won't feel as though you really belong socially — which is very hard on humans, separate as they tend to feel from others, right from birth. Even worse will be the spiritual loneliness. Your part of earth may feel like a dark hole, a place where the people you meet have no conscious connection to God.

I ask, "Doesn't earth usually feel like that? Isn't that partly how we evolve by incarnating there? Like you said, 'Low and slow and dull.'"

Although I don't have to tell Merlin, or seem to brag in front of the group, I've already been to earth for many thousands of lifetimes. Dim but sure, memory reminds me of Earth's distinctive heaviness and, especially, the terrible and pervasive sense of being cut off from God: like gravity, only personal. Separation kicks you right in your most tender place, not *the nuts* or *the tits* but your soul.

Merlin answers, *YOU know very well, there are degrees of feeling cut off from God. I'm warning YOU. This will be the worst YOU have ever had.*

"Aw, come on, Merlin," I try to joke. "All my past incarnations are hanging around me, right now. You can see them as clear as haloes: loads of times, I've felt completely cut off from God and, always, I survived it.

Of course, Merlin and I both know about the one awful exception, my life in Atlantis when things went horribly wrong, when I wound up watching the crashes and feeling the screams, accepting the terrible truth, that every single volunteer on that project — not just me — oh, collectively we had failed.

Such a spectacular failure! I still remember every smash of a building and every single death scream. They landed within my memory like personal failures. Even after lifting out of my dead Atlantean body, I stayed around for years of earth time, obsessively engaged in a grim-and-ghostly watching.

How come? Because I felt obligated to own every bit of that destruction and, personally, suffer in penance for our project's terrible failure. Failure as big as could be. And irrevocable, for all time.

Teasing Merlin (kinda) I say, "Honestly, you know everything I've been through. Give me some credit. Why would you need to warn me like this? Are you trying to scare me off?"

Merlin turns slightly stiff. Maybe that's because he hasn't incarnated as human for such a long time, but right now the guy seems to have no sense of humor. Dignity is what he has instead. Gravitas. That I can feel for sure, because suddenly Merlin has grown serious like a perfect Greek hero, a statue sculpted in marble.

Out of compassion, I've been warning YOU gently. Now I'm asking YOU to hear this plainly. Even by your standards, this will be rough.

Slow down and listen. About your particular Life Contract, for close to 20 years of earth time, YOU will see very few flashes of spiritual light, until you feel as though being buried alive, with all of your personal light nearly extinguished.

Typically for Life Contracts of the Awakening Project, YOU will grow up in a family that lives in complete spiritual darkness. Not only because they've forgotten the purpose of their lives, but because they've become addicted to favorite consolations that distract them from despair.

Consequently, these good souls will seem stuck beyond stuck, with no idea what they're missing and scant desire to find out. True, those next parents of yours, Ernie and Sue, they mean well. They will be diligent parents, loving YOU and trying their very best. But consider, will YOU be able to accept their love, when realizing within your soul how they are stuck beyond stuck?

Right now, this doesn't strike me as a big deal. My glowy, sparkling energy body gives Merlin the equivalent of a shrug, as if to say, "Come on, quit making such a fuss. I can handle this."

Instantly, Merlin moves closer, like right in my face.

Don't be so quick, don't be so sure.

Let me remind you, for many lifetimes YOU incarnated to serve humanity in ways that seemed noble, given your dreams. Other lifetimes, YOU agreed to suffer in order to gain specific kinds of knowledge for the sake of greater service later. By contrast, this particular childhood will terrify YOU to the core with its meaninglessness. Even though your circumstances are physically secure, and seem pleasant enough....

No exaggeration, YOU could go for many years before meeting a single person who's spiritually awake inside, nobody, not even a little. I'll say that again. Not a single adult who crosses your path will care to connect to God. Not one single adult.

Living among these people, understandably, you'll start to identify with them. It will seem inevitable that YOU will lose your light. Completely gone. Full blackout.

Understand this? Because once YOU agree to this Life Contract, free will won't be able to stop any of this from happening.   No exaggeration: All of YOUR spiritual light will be covered in mud, barely recognizable; and the same for most of YOUR talents.

For a moment, a flicker goes through me, like a candle flame briefly stopped by the wind. In human terms, maybe this would look like a shudder.

"You don't mean that I will actually lose my connection to spiritual light, do you?"

Never, Merlin says. *That cannot be. However, YOU will feel as if all that light has been lost.*

And remember how Earth's illusions include being stuck in a heavy reality? Often YOU have chosen lifetimes as a spiritual teacher. Typically, this has come at the expense of enjoying the human part of Earth School, simple pleasures like eating and playing and aimlessly spending time with others.

Well, that's the best life will offer YOU. No kidding, the best. For years. Except for small flashes of talent.

Do not underestimate this challenge: eating and playing aimlessly, while hanging out with people who are shut off from their spiritual light.

"That's it? That's all you've got?" Practically giggling, I say, "So I'm gonna waste a little time by playing? Seems easy enough." My radiating light sends out marigold pulsations of anticipation.

Merlin's light brightens, if possible.

Yes, this lifetime could be very good for YOU, once you get over the spiritual blackout. The point of this Awakening Project is contrast.

Eventually, YOU can wake up to your light. Bit by bit, reviving your spiritual connection, YOU may even gain the new kind of Enlightenment available after the Shift, Age of Awakening Enlightenment. Certainly, YOU'll become far more awake than ever before, despite all your long history as a soul.

With these words, Merlin has clinched the choice for me. Can he tell? Of course. So now he turns toward the assembled group, once again broadcasting strongly to all of us (not only me).

Remember, many other souls will be doing the exact same thing. On this mission each of you will serve as an Awakener. *Everyone on the Awakening Project will, basically, do that same job.*

Imagine, hundreds of thousands of you to be born either shortly before or after the Shift. Born as Awakeners, bright spiritual lights who feel demoted, and can't remember why.

Isolated from others around you; dimly remembering joy while living in the spiritual equivalent of a black hole: Thousands of you brave Awakeners, you'll be grieving and yet unable to grieve, lacking any clear understanding of what is gone.

Suffering a terrible sorrow without any name! While we're still here in this heaven, how can I prepare you for this sense of loss? Impossible, except that I can tell you this. It will be especially hard to not be able to put into words... what exactly you've lost.

But hear this as well: one by one, every single one of you Awakeners can reclaim your light. Every one of you can regain it. Waking up, gradually, you can awaken as much joy as you have ever known on earth; all that joy and more, until you are living with your full spiritual light.

To illustrate, the small pushpins on my map go from shiny black to shimmering gold.

I look with wonder and then I make use of a certain kind of switch built into each of us souls, always available while we are angels. I pause that instant of wonder, banging around in it for a miniature eternity. Merlin continues.

*What will happen when so many Awakeners do the very same thing, around the same time, in a newly transformed world? According to our plan, this will set up a rhythm, because so many souls are going from **no light** to **full light**.*

*Energetically this can entrain other souls who seek spiritual evolution. You'll make it exceptionally easy for them to do a similar wake-up, hitch-hiking onto this **Awakeners' Blessing** which helps to bring truth into earth.*

Millions can move into Enlightenment and live That. They'll be able to live in Age of Awakening Enlightenment, a distinctively new way to be one with God, quite different from Traditional Enlightenment. This great new potential for evolution will start up during your lifetime.

Although all of you here have served on earth many times, know this. In many respects, this will be like constructing a different planet. Doing your humble, human best, becoming a bringer of the Awakener's Blessing, you can actively help to transform the destinies of innumerable souls.

Think of it. Helping so many beautiful beings, younger in soul age than you, and firmly stuck on the wheel of rebirth. Also helping so many middle-aged souls. And even helping old souls, who have struggled for lifetimes to fully accept themselves and live with God while on earth.

"Did you say that even the youngest souls will be able to gain Enlightenment too?"

Possibilities make my head start to spin. Literally. Around here, sometimes that happens; it feels like tickling.

Exactly. Every human will get to choose. Absolutely everyone, at any level of evolution, will be able to choose Enlightenment. What will set that in motion? Simply one small request from inside – and then that soul will start quickening its pace of growth, evolving extra-fast. One human day at a time, they'll discover how, in this second era on earth, self-realization will no longer demand a monastic-style renunciation.

All this will become possible, and why? Because so many of you Awakeners will have made the journey from utter spiritual darkness into radiant light. Each of you can inspire through how you have shaped your personal journey.

Exponentially augmenting those personal triumphs, the collective power of the huge Awakening Project, at this unique time in earth's history, will create a momentum of its own.

Quick as the ring of a tiny bell, I remember some of my own past hard-won lessons, learned over the lifetimes: Stay brave. Use my power. Lose gracefully. Be patient.

I realize that Merlin was right, too, about my longstanding snobbery over *dumb human pleasures.* Guess I'll finally have incentive to grow past that one!

By now, Merlin's telepathic voice rings with a contagious excitement.

Join in the work of the Awakeners. Help to make the most of this unique time on earth. Help any soul who desires to make The Great Leap. And the more the merrier, the more the easier.

Suddenly our map changes. The dots themselves haven't changed. They're still gold, but while seeing them I realize that soon **I *will* become one of them!**

All along, America's background color has been colored a dark gray. Has something changed? Because it dawns on me now, this gray background color is really made of innumerable dots.

As I watch, fascinated, what happens? More and more of these darkish dots begin turn to gold.

And then the map expands until the whole world comes into view. No longer just an enlarged map of the U.S.A., I'm seeing all the nations of earth. Bursts of gold grow distinct, then flow and shine. Gradually I realize what exactly I'm seeing, no less than earth producing spiritual fireworks. Only these fireworks shine on land… instead of the sky or, even, a heaven.

Nobody's speaking now, neither Merlin, nor anyone else. And then all of us hear it, ringing far lower and louder than any mere bell, more like the most immense chime imaginable. God's voice. All of us at this Planning Meeting can hear God speaking out of the twinkling air.

He says just one thing:

WHEN THIS HAPPENS, I WILL BE SO HAPPY.

If I had eyes, I would weep for joy. If I had a heart, it would be praying. All of me is shouting and singing and sobbing, all at once. Of course my answer goes, "Yes. Please, yes. Let me help Your earth to take this Great Leap. And I promise, I'll give this everything I've got. Bring me there."

PART TWO. Exactly Who I'm Supposed to Be

CHAPTER 8.

The Most Delicious Ice Cream Ever

"Wake up, Laura," says a nurse. I wake up, then fall back to sleep, pushing my head firmly into the pillow. Almost as if I can smile with my whole head, not just my mouth.

Soon after, I'm drinking water through a clever sort of tube called a straw. New and fun! I can sort of remember where I've been, something about going to my real home. Bigger colors somehow, that's what I remember best. How I wish I could see those colors again, so much clearer than what we have here. And prettier. And so many more of them.

Guess I fall asleep again, because next thing I know, Mommy wakes me up. I smile to see her again. Her eyes are big and brown and beautiful. Although I don't remember why, exactly, I have a new kind of good feeling about this mother of mine. She is exactly who she is supposed to be. And so am I.

For the first time, when Mommy hugs me, I can feel that she really does love me.

"How's my sweet baby?" she asks.

It has been so long since anybody called me that, any kind of a baby. I snuggle right up to my Mommy.

She drives me home. Along the way she tells me the operation was a complete success. No longer will I get sick over every little thing. In September, I can go to school, first grade. I won't have to miss school like I used to because, from now on, I will be strong, healthy and strong.

All this turns out to be true. But the main thing is how happy I feel now, like somebody gave me a new kind of *safe feeling* that will be inside of me for keeps. Another good part is all that ice cream. My first meal back home is a great big bowl of orange sherbet.

CHAPTER 9

Eating Cherries Like Kings

On this sunny morning, I'm walking to school, walking across a huge, long field. This walking is special because I'm on grass instead of the crumbly-looking, gray rug we have at home.

Why is it, when walking with grownups, I never notice things like this? I mean, the *Trust me, I'm the ground* kind of smell of the grass. It's so familiar, like a perfume hidden inside the sweat of my fingers when I try sniffing them now.

I think, dirt brown is becoming my new favorite color. Since I'm a schoolgirl now, I can give myself things like a Favorite Color.

Seems like whatever I see or touch is just like a schoolgirl present that gives itself to me, a thrilling new toy that I receive just for paying attention. Well, like my Mommy says many times each day, "That's life."

Walking and walking, I realize how special dirt is. For one thing it gets more magical the longer I smell it. But really, lucky me, lately any way that I breathe feels like a treat.

Everybody knows how smell works, so the grownups don't even bother to tell you… how the new morning air each day is like having somebody give you a present, only instead of special giftwrap and a bow, your new present could be wrapped up in anything at all, like a smell or a color or tiny little sounds that get bigger simply because you like them.

For example, I really like my new school shoes, called *Saddle Shoes*. Although they have a very disappointing name because they don't come with a horse, unless you count my feet, which cannot be a horse, obviously! Back at sounds, it's such fun how my shoes can make hilarious scuffling noises, simply because of whichever way I walk in them, kicking up dirt.

Oh, I've been feeling so great ever since my birthday operation. Ever since coming back from the hospital, I haven't been sick a single day. It's the best, being a big girl who can walk all by myself for this entire trip to school. Other children my age are making the same magical walk. "Two grownup-sized blocks," Mommy calls it, which doesn't explain the thrill of seeing other kids walking too, coming from their own faraway homes. It's like we all belong to something together. This, I guess, is the meaning of going to school.

When it was my first day of school, Mommy took me by the hand and showed me the way. Now, because I'm such a big girl, she lets me walk on my own. It was such a proud day when my parents gave me my school bag, an important thing to carry when going out into the world. My school bag is brown leather, and I love it very much.

I also love being able to take a walk in nature, like I'm doing now. Mommy and Daddy explained it to me, how we have moved away from The City to Glen Oaks in Queens, where we live in a garden apartment. It even has a backyard, which makes us much closer to nature than when we lived in The City.

In this apartment, we live downstairs. Upstairs is my friend Johnny, who has a big smile. He is just my age, smart and funny at "Age 6, going on 16," says my mother. She has a best friend now, Johnny's Mommy. Together they have coffee klatches while I play with Johnny and, meanwhile, little baby Amy is not in the way since she can play with Johnny's annoying baby sister Gina. So everything is exactly wonderful.

School is easy. Of course, I want more, more, more, because our reader is so easy. Teacher won't let me have a different one, even though I told her that I've been reading for two years already.

Teacher doesn't believe me and, also, she says school readers are better for me than what I pretended to read at home and, also, who do I think I am, anyway? If I can't change readers, I wish that at least I could be the teacher. I'm sure I could do that, only teacher won't let me stand in front of the group and play teacher.

I tried. She didn't like it. Then I had to go out and stand in the hall. By now what I like most about school is walking across the big field. Also, I like coming home from school and playing at home any way I want. And, of course, what I like best is when Daddy comes home from work.

Mommy is lots of fun lately, because Amy has caught up just fine. She has become an "adorable toddler" who made a necklace from shoelaces and big beads made of wood, bright red and yellow and blue, like the balloons on our packages of Wonder Bread. Amy gets to wear this necklace of hers. I think it's annoying how she wears that necklace all the time.

Mommy loves both of her daughters exactly the same. She has explained this to us. Not having favorites is part of being a good parent, which is what she and Daddy always do. Sometimes she talks about how hard it was for her when she was my age, because her Step-Mommy Leah didn't love her. Grandpa Julius wasn't at home much, because he was busy becoming a millionaire at the factory.

All this was very hard for Mommy and her two sisters, but especially not having love was hard. For that reason Mommy is sure to tell us every day how much she loves us. My job is to tell her back, "I love you, Mommy. I love you so much." Hearing this makes her happier than anything. We hug a lot, too.

When Daddy comes home from work, all of us hug even more. Then Daddy puts new music on the record player, because we must always have music. It's like cigarettes, always there, only I really like the music. From listening to those records, I have learned grownup songs, like I can sing "If you want to know who we are, we are gentlemen of Japan." That is the first song I learned from a record, one of our Gilbert and Sullivan songs.

When we eat dinner, it is a happy time. Bath is okay. I'm scared to go to sleep, though. To cheer me up, Mommy and Daddy have taught me to fold my hands in a special prayer way and say this:

Now I lay me down to sleep.

I pray the Lord my soul to keep.

If I should die before I wake

I pray the Lord my soul to take.

Then I'm supposed to ask God to bless people. Mommy and Daddy give me names to say for that part, like them and Aunt Carol and Cousin Jay and poor Aunt Elly, who has an emotional illness. Although this prayer is supposed to comfort me, it scares me more than I used to feel before learning that "helpful" prayer. "If I should die before I wake?" What on earth is that supposed to mean?

This prayer, which I'm expected to say whether I want to or not, it's the only way to talk to God that my parents have ever mentioned, so maybe it's the only prayer in all the world.

Well, here's the best thing I can say about that prayer. It has given a name to my fear. No longer am I scared of monsters under my bed. Because of this prayer I'm more terrified about what will happen tonight, or some other night. What if, after I fall asleep, I will not wake up again but be dead? If that doesn't wind up happening, I sure wish I would grow up already. Daddy says that when I grow up, I won't be so scared. We'll see. This fearless grownup thing may not be true for everyone, because Mommy is scared about many things, which she calls *My Phobias* -- like being scared in elevators and never taking the subway but always having to drive her car instead.

Anyway, I like it best when I have special adventures with Daddy, who doesn't have phobias and is almost always happy. He has smart green eyes that shine with light beams, kind of like the sun. Today we're going to have a special treat. It is a beautiful Friday in May, and my father gives me permission to play hooky from school, just for one day, which will be allowed because he says I may have this special treat.

For starters, we ride the subway together. It's my first time, and I love it. A subway train is like a big noisy city hidden under the ground. Once we're riding, my Pop prepares me to visit his office for the first time, so he tells me something very special, all about his new job.

You see, Questing Reader, my Daddy has just started a business. A new one. Why did he have to do that? He explains, after The War he went back to school, like the way I am going to school now, only my school is Public School 186 and his school was called City College.

Before The War he went there and studied Chemistry. Except later he changed his mind, which is how he wound up graduating with a Bachelor of *Science* degree as an *English* major. Silly but he couldn't help it. The sad part was how his father, my Grandpa Hugo, thought this mixed-up degree was no good. But my father says he was proud of himself anyway, even if nobody else in the family tells him so, because he was the first one in his family to get a college degree, the first person ever.

I love learning about the world and life, so I ask my father to tell me more stories, and he does. So many things that I didn't know before! For instance, when I was born, my father provided for the family by writing for a newspaper called *Daily News*. But they broke his heart, Daddy said.

Because his job was to write about the United Nations. Every day he would write a story about this wonderful place, U.N. for short, and how it was bringing hope to the world. But then a stinky editor at the newspaper would take his story and make it seem like the U.N. was stupid. When Daddy would read the version of his story in print, he wanted to scream. He wanted to never write another word again.

When enough was enough, he quit. Grandpa Julius gave him some old printing equipment from the basement of his big house, which Daddy used to start a printing business. Only that business went bad. Soon he became bankrupt, which was very serious. Afterward he had to find something new. Around when little Amy was born, my father had a lightbulb idea. Because somebody told him about a business called Fashion Models. And then he learned more, until he invented something new to help the models advertise, something he named *Composites*.

Composites were a new way for a model to advertise, because a composite would show a collection of the model's best pictures. What else was listed there? The composite gave important facts for hiring each model, like her rate per hour. All this information would fit on just one sheet of paper.

Daddy said that making this new business was like becoming a pioneer, and he wouldn't be satisfied only to make the first composites, no no! My Daddy was going to make the best ones in the entire world. Zenith Press was his name for this business.

Despite being new, this was going to be really successful and support our family, I'd see.

On our way to this new office, we change subway trains and ride some more. Then we some stairs take us onto the street, so we can walk down Broadway.

Stores are sprinkled all over the block; really, sprinkled; as if I were playing in a sandbox and sprinkled a whole line of sand puddles in a row, and every single one came to life as a store. Besides that, I find so many people, cars, taxis, windows, you-name-its. All that traffic makes the street noisy and exciting; also smelly, but only in the most interesting ways.

Inside Daddy's office building, we get to ride an elevator for the first time. At least, it's the first time for me. What a big, clanky box! I am allowed to push the button. After we get outside the elevator, it is a little like Grandma and Grandpa's building, with little apartments inside. Only these are offices for business, not places to live, like apartments.

Machines are in Daddy's office, machines for typing and adding; also, the office has a table with a big board especially for doing layouts and mechanicals. These are like my father's favorite toys at work, helping him get composites ready to go to a printer. On his desk I see a heavy black telephone, just like the one we have at home. Otherwise, everything else in that office is totally different from home.

Squares of color are on the floor, made of shiny linoleum. And you can see an extra-big window on one wall, but when you look out through that window, guess what you see. The sky? Children playing?

No, there's nothing to see but a brick wall. I laugh at this funny, ridiculous joke, which makes Daddy smile with a kind of surprise like he just realized that I'm right, it is pretty funny.

Then he explains how those bricks out the window belong to another office building, a lot like his, except not as special.

He's telling me so many grownup things to understand all at once. What matters most? Inside this building is Daddy's office, where he is going to help a lot of models, and make lots of money, and have oodles of fun. While Daddy explains all this, his voice sounds excited. His eyes look scared, though. So, I throw my arms around him, hugging him extra tight, and tell him that I am excited too. His business is going to be wonderful, just like the United Nations. And no stinky editor is going to make it go all backward, either.

"You're going to be proud of me some day," he says.

I say, "Of course," and hug him some more.

Then my Daddy, Ernie Rosenbaum, tells me some news that is even more exciting. Right now, he is going to take us on a special fun trip. To the Empire State Building, that's where. It is the tallest building in all of New York. After walking there, we go up a *really* big elevator, even fancier than the one at Zenith Press. On the long ride up, we see loads of people, and a pretty lady in a uniform makes the elevator go, until we arrive at the top.

Many people are there already, but my father knows his way around, so he leads me through the crowd to somewhere special. It's the best place for looking all the way down at the street. Held in the arms of my big, strong father, I'm shown all the tiny people below. Then he points out tiny little taxis picking them up, busy little toy cars, like the most wonderful game you could ever buy.

To my amazement, Daddy explains that all those miniature cars and people are real. Actually, they are the same as what we saw when we were walking outside, before we went up so high in the elevator. When you are on the ground, people look big, especially the grownups. But when you go high enough, you have "perspective," Daddy tells me; and then he says the most amazing thing, that you can also give yourself perspective, and not just while you're at the Empire State Building.

I can tell he's teaching me now. "Never forget this," he says. "In life, you must do everything for yourself and that includes deciding things for yourself. You can choose your own perspective.

"For instance, some people believe in a God who fixes everything for you, but your Mommy and I don't believe in that. We are agnostics, which means we don't sit waiting around for God to rescue us. We must do things for ourselves. You can learn to do that, too."

Wow! I'm not sure if I understand that last grownup part he said, but I know that I will never forget seeing all those teeny, tiny people. Next, we take the elevator down, down, down. Once we're out on the street again, the people turn normal-sized, which is kind of a relief.

Then, for an extra treat, Daddy takes me for a walk on Fifth Avenue, where people are dressed up really fancy. When a street vendor walks by, my father buys us a bag of cherries. Down the street we go, pulling sweet, red cherries out of the brown paper bag and eating them one by one.

What do you do with the pits? Daddy shows me how you can spit them out, right on the street, and then reach for a shiny new cherry. Down Fifth Avenue we go, eating cherries and spitting their pits onto the pavement. Today I have also seen teeny, tiny people and cars. It's a day I will never forget. Holding my Daddy's hand, I feel like we have become King and Queen of the whole world.

CHAPTER 10

Please, No More Hokey Pokey

Moving to a new apartment complex in Queens, it's amazing how huge this building is, shaped like a low, wide U; slicing a city block in half the long way, and completely filling that entire long half. Our building is made of bricks, surely solid enough to scare away any big bad wolf.

One tree stands to the left side of the U, while a matching tree stands to the right. These are the most enormous trees anywhere.

Mommy calls our wrap-around building a courtyard because it contains entrances to seven different apartment buildings. Mysteriously! What's inside all those connected bricks? To find out you walk through one of the seven main doors. Right at the entrance, you'll find all the mailboxes for that whole building. If you keep on exploring and go up the stairs, you'll find three locked doors on every floor. Altogether, each building has four stories with three apartments each.

Strangers might see that U-shape and think it is all one building, maybe with every apartment connected to all the neighbors, with everybody like best friends. Pretty funny, when you think about it, how different this place really is! Still, it's a wonderland, with a bristly greenish lawn for playing and so many kids to play with.

In the center of the courtyard are benches where mothers sit, talking about important things that only grownups can understand. Out the corners of their eyes, they watch children like me, playing with our bright pink Spaldeen balls. The bench mothers wear short shorts and colorful blouses that look pointy in front. They talk a lot. They look alike, too, with short hair and red-red lipstick and cigarettes for puffing. Weather permitting, every Mommy works hard on her tan.

By now I'm a big girl of seven, so I know words like *weather permitting*. By now I know so much about life, living in a big four-story building that's packed with children my age. We Rosenbaums live in 3B. To get there you must take that long staircase I already told you about, Questing Reader.

Such a wonderland building, really! That staircase is a big toy in itself. I get to run up and down as much as I want. After living here a while, I meet all the girls in my building. Here's who they are:

➤ Karen lives on the first floor. She's just my age, and walks with me to the new school, P.S. 164.
➤ Her next-door neighbor Annette doesn't have a father, just a Mommy and an annoying baby brother. Besides English, sometimes they speak French. Speak it very fast!
➤ On the second floor lives Maureen, who is fun, although she also has an annoying little brother.
➤ Christine lives on that same floor, in the apartment just below ours; and let me tell you, they are noisy people, especially when her Daddy starts hitting the kids. Did I mention? Christine has two annoying baby brothers.
➤ Above us, on the fourth floor, lives Sachiko with her parents. They speak Japanese and seem very quiet. Maybe that's because Sachiko doesn't have any annoying little children in her family. Lucky girl!
➤ Finally, next to me lives Nora, a beautiful girl who's a couple years older. When Nora's father gets drunk, he

throws her out into the hallway, so that's how I get to know her.

Come to think of it, many fathers in my building get drunk. When I pass them on the stairway, I recognize a certain smell, like old shoes and misery. Even if my nose wasn't working right, how else could I tell? From the screaming, of course. The drunks get so angry and, like Mommy says, the walls are paper thin.

Being Laura is so much nicer than life for most of the other girls in my building, because my parents don't get drunk, and it's also pretty nice that I don't have any pesky little brothers. However, I sure wish that I could have a wonderful brother of my own, a big brother who would tell me what life is about and what exactly I'm supposed to be learning.

Preferably he would be strong and kind, just a couple years older than me. Otherwise, I doubt that I'll ever manage to figure it out, how to grow up. What if all the other kids in my building grow up except me? When I think about how much I don't understand about growing up, this is a terrible feeling, sad and scary and lonely. Meanwhile, I do learn about going to school. Karen walks with me, there and back, every school day. Going to second grade, P.S. 164, what an adventure!

It's half a mile away, which means blocks and blocks, walking past little stores (especially interesting are the two candy stores), and then crossing many streets with apartment buildings; until there we are, at a huge public school. Much larger than my old one, I guess.

Actually, this school might just seem bigger, since here we do something very special after lunch break. At P.S. 164, everybody goes home for lunch. After you have your sandwich with Mommy, you walk back to school and wait for classes to start. You must sit quietly in the biggest room ever, an auditorium, with a high stage in the front. Sitting in this room we are *In Assembly*, Karen tells me. There we sit, each school day, waiting for afternoon classes to start. During Assembly after lunch, we always have a talent show. First, we sing certain songs together. Following that, kids sing solos, standing up high, on the stage. Most popular for our group singing *is I've Been Working on the Railroad*. I'm not quite sure what a railroad is, which embarrasses me because it seems like everybody else knows, since they're singing with loud, confident voices.

As for the part about "Dinah, blow your horn," this really seems peculiar, because who is this kid, Dinah? And why does she carry a horn? And how come the grownups let her make noise on the train, instead of shushing her up? And, especially, why do they keep encouraging her to make extra noise with this horn? Isn't her voice loud enough? That Dinah must have very different parents from anybody I've ever met.

School includes other embarrassing things like that. For instance, seems like almost every day, my second- grade teacher makes us do a kind of dance called *The Hokey Pokey*:

You put your right foot in

You take your right foot out

You put your right foot in

And you shake it all about

You do the hokey pokey

And you turn yourself around

That's what it's all about.

To me it is stupid, being forced to move parts of my private, personal body in front of the other children. But that's not even the worst part. Such troubling words: "That's what it's all about"!

You see, every day of my life, for as long as I can remember, I keep asking myself the same question, a question I don't even know the words for exactly, but it's a question that could be called, "What's it all about?" Finally, in school, this idiotic song has given me an answer to my burning question, only wouldn't you know it? Their answer just has to be wrong. Because how would moving your right foot or your "whole self" into a circle — this clumsy show-off dancing which isn't even graceful like dancing is supposed to be — how would moving parts of your body just because teacher says so… how is this ever, ever supposed to explain to me what life is all about?

So embarrassing, and even scary! Could the Hokey Pokey really be It? And if not, will I ever meet anybody who tells me the truth?

Of course, going to school does include other parts that are just wonderful, like the many new smells: clay and school paper and freshly sharpened pencils. Oh, oh, and there's this wonderful part: standing in line with the other kids, when all of us smell so great. Because I guess everybody knows, there can never be a better smell for a person than when a kid is six or seven years old. Except when you put a whole bunch of us kids all together in a line.

At school, we're supposed to stand in size places but, to me, how tall we look isn't the interesting part. Instead, standing in line makes my nose so happy, it feels like having a picnic. Standing in line reminds me of one of my favorite toys, a xylophone. You know how a xylophone has keys you can bang on? And each key is painted a different color, so shiny. And isn't it amazing how well they are made? Because each note matches its shiny color just perfectly.

At school we're supposed to be good children and always and line up, even while standing still and looking straight ahead, guess what? I can travel in my imagination, going up or down the row, pausing to smell each kid and also feel the boy's or girl's energy. It's at least as much fun as any xylophone.

School is like that. Now that I'm a big girl, toys aren't obvious, but you can find them wherever you go. Also, every morning school starts with an amazing toy, the principal's intercom, which brings us a different kind of Assembly.

Playing with this toy, our principal talks to us from far away, but it sounds like he's right in our classroom. Although we can't see him with our eyes, that doesn't matter to me, because I don't usually pay much attention to how things look anyway; not when I can feel the person's energy, or recognize how somebody feels to my heart. Plus, for me, the voice alone is all you need to find out what's going on with another person.

Take my principal for example. I don't think I've ever seen face to face, but I sure know him well from his voice on the intercom. Our principal is very old, of course, and he knows what children need, although he remembers nothing whatsoever about being a child. Still, his job is to make us understand how to become grownups like him, which means to be good and obedient. If we would only do that simple thing, we can grow up just fine.

Every Tuesday, the principal reads us a list of words for a spelling test, which is given at the same time to every single child in every single classroom. Afterward, we turn in test papers to teacher, and somehow the principal finds out what every one of us wrote. To me this is proof that he knows every single thing that happens to every child in the entire school.

One of these spelling tests is a big deal to me, because it includes the word *synonym*. Somehow, I know that word, maybe because I've been reading at home for so many years now, and Mommy helps me to take home piles of books from the library. No wonder I know how to spell synonym on that spelling test, so I do, and then on Wednesday, what a surprise!

As usual, the principal tells us how to spell every word on the spelling test. Only this time he announces that only two students in the whole school were able to spell it correctly. After the intercom assembly is over, I keep waiting for my teacher to tell the class, "Good girl, Laura. You are one of those two students. Clap for her, everybody."

Only that never happens, so I save up my tears until I can go home and cry, like Mommy has taught me to do. Teacher often asks us to clap for different students, so why doesn't she ever, ever let the whole class clap for me?

When I'm promoted the next year, I hope my third grade teacher will be nicer. Only she turns out to be just as bad as the one in second grade. Between classes I still have lots of fun, but during classes, oboy, my teacher treats me like some kind of troublemaker.

Every day in this classroom, what happens? She'll ask a question and up goes my hand instantly. Only does she call on me? Almost never. Even though I try raising my hand in different ways, the patient way with my hand sticking up like a tree, and plenty of other ways; even the exciting windmill way where I shake my hand at the wrist, going faster and faster and faster. None of it matters. How come she doesn't like to call on me?

Except one day she does. She tells me to come over to her desk. Then Teacher talks to me about my bad behavior with being impatient and raising my hand so much. And I can't help but cry a little, although trying not to, and finally I look right into her eyes and ask her, "Why won't you call on me?"

A wise look comes onto Teacher's face then, a look I've seen on her many times, like she's holding a tiny smile inside her lips. It's her special teacher's face about being grownup and beautiful and good to every single child. Teacher makes that face for me now, and then she starts talking in a funny voice, as if she has practiced in advance which words she will use.

"You must understand. You are not the only child in my classroom. I must give every single child a chance to answer my questions. When you try to answer more than your share, I must ignore you so that you can learn this important lesson."

Oh, how I wish for an older brother, so that he could help me to know which lessons I'm supposed to be learning. Preferably in advance, not after I have made mistakes without knowing better. Worst of all is being treated as though I should have known everything all along.

CHAPTER 11

Find Your Own Fun

My parents never do supply me with an older brother. Although they provide everything else that I ask for and I'll admit, over the years, Sue and Ernie teach me a big secret of growing up. "That's life. C'est la vie! Find your own fun."

Questing Reader, before I move up to the next big step in my story, at age nine, how about this? I want to tell you more about what it's like being raised at 141-33 78th Avenue, Flushing, Queens. Actually, I wind up living in that same apartment until I leave for college. Physically, I'm given such a stable and comfortable childhood!

Our forever apartment has three bedrooms. That means one each for my sister, the parents, and me. Our black-and-white television is kept in my parents' bedroom, where I can come in and watch shows whenever I like because, as they've told me proudly, "Our door is always open."

In the small kitchen, Mommy dishes out meals that I adore, with sweet snacks always available. A distinctive blend of Food Heaven and Food Hell, that's my kitchen, because it's as if angels beg me to eat ice cream for breakfast but I'm also spooked by a terror of growing fat.

Apart from the general culture of worrying, why does food seem like such a constant danger, rivalling my other big fear, going crazy? That's because my Daddy can often be found alone in the kitchen, standing in front of the open ice box — that's what my mother calls it, remembering the real ice box from her childhood, when an ice man would come regularly.

Sigh! I'll walk into the living room, see the kitchen off to the side, and there's my Daddy, standing in front of that tall, open ice box with all the food in it. As I'd come to describe it in later years, Dad would download food straight into his body. However, no playful reference to the future can change the misery that I see daily, my Daddy stuffing himself with food and not being able to stop.

At a time when few Americans are seriously overweight, my father stands at 5 feet, 5 inches, weighing 250 pounds. He struggles to diet. Every day he loses that battle, especially while standing in front of the fridge. Where, incidentally, his naked misery often includes literally being naked — see House Rule #4, toward the end of this chapter.

But kitchen worries don't spill out into our living room, at least not for me, not often anyway. You see, our "living room" is mostly our music room, centering around a state-of-the-art record player. Nearby you see huge shelves; crammed from floor to ceiling with long-playing records, black vinyl inside clever, colorful jackets; and next to our record player is the best part, the ever-changing piles of my Dad's latest favorites, stacked neatly next to the turntable.

Like a merry-go-round for your ears, that turntable spins around, playing music whenever Mr. Music is home: records galore, with Daddy buying more every Friday. Although every form of music delights him, he loves jazz most of all.

Questing Reader, have you ever seen the Sesame Street classic, *Put Down the Ducky*? It's a parody of music at Birdland, THE best nightclub for jazz in the world. Ernie became a regular, not that he talked much about that at home. Sue didn't mention it either, not until I was all grown up, and then she told me about it, laughing affectionately.

"Ernie insisted on going there, which drove me crazy. You know, people were always getting murdered at Birdland. Maybe because they kept it dark, for atmosphere. Okay, possibly Birdland had that problem with murders because of the darkness but it could also have been due to the drugs a lot of the musicians took, or maybe the big problem was all the gangsters who came.

"What can I tell you for sure? Whenever your Dad would call to say he was going to Birdland after work, all night I'd be worried sick. Worried sick every single minute, until he came home. And it didn't ease my mind how sometimes while he was there, news would come on the radio, 'There's been another killing at Birdland.'

"But what could I do? Ernie loved it."

Sometimes, hearing other kids talk at school, I learn that other families go to church, or do sports, or join the P.T.A., or somehow belong to something. Not us, though. My parents belong to nothing except for that secret place, Birdland. Whenever I ask if we could belong to something, my parents look very proud of themselves, shaking their heads as if saying "No. We think for ourselves, that's why. Intellectuals like us don't join things. We entertain."

However, Mommy does pay for me to take ballet lessons while I'm in third grade; a lot of girls do that, so why not me? Ballet class strikes me as strange, neither joining anything exactly nor being in school. My teacher, Mademoiselle, is sweet and graceful. She's very patient, while teaching my friend Karen from the first floor, and me, and a few other girls from the neighborhood.

Except I feel so awkward, not at all like a beautiful ballerina. Mostly I have a problem because my *turnout* is next to zero. It's very embarrassing how my First Position looks so much like my Third Position or my Fifth Position. Truth be told, my version of all five ballet positions looks like, "Standing self-consciously with my feet sticking out in whichever direction."

An altogether different kind of awkwardness happens one day, while Mademoiselle is showing us how to extend our arms. Suddenly she stares at how I'm holding my hands, and a flash of excitement makes her eyes glow — as if her eyes open up within her eyes. In a manner totally different from any other time while teaching our class, Mademoiselle runs over to me and says:

"Your hands, the way you are holding your hands! It's exactly like a real ballerina. How did you learn to do that?"

She's practically touching my right hand, as if it has become a treasure -- causing me to feel incredibly embarrassed, self-conscious, too. And then a weird thought comes to me, like from the back of my brain. A quiet but stern voice reminds me, "In this lifetime you're not supposed to know how to do that."

Quickly I snap back to my senses, with my pudgy little body standing there in the room as I stare back at Mademoiselle, and then both of us look at my hand. Instantly that goes all clunky and graceless and stiff, like a typical eight-year-old in her little ballet class where she's no good at dancing at all.

Mademoiselle returns to the front of the room and, rather than feeling complimented, I feel worse as a dancer than usual, and as if I just broke some rule that I was supposed to remember. Never again do I move my arms or feet in any way that's remarkable. Soon the series of classes ends, not to be continued, and somehow that makes me feel relieved more than anything else.

So what if I'm not good at ballet? Who needs outside activities? Especially when you live in a building full of little girls just your age. Besides, maybe my parents have a point when they tell me that smart people like us don't join things. All that we Rosenbaums do is entertain.

Really, it's fun when my parents have company. Mommy serves us delicious meals that she has prepared with special care. Entertaining company also means perfect music selected by my father, and all the grownups are talking and laughing and drinking red wine from Italy.

Who comes to visit? Daddy's friends from Manhattan come to visit, friends that he meets through work. I'll fall asleep listening to everyone's stories through my bedroom door. Just one example: Ray is a photographer who likes to keep unusual pets.

First, he tries a skunk, but that pet ruins his linoleum floor. So then Ray gets a rooster, and now he has a great time because his pet helps him to live as a swinging homosexual in the City.

How exactly? Ray explains how every day he walks his rooster on a leash, like a dog, and whenever he sees a good-looking guy, ha! Ray will stroll over casually and deliver his line that always starts a great conversation. "Hello. Want to meet my cock? His name is Lucky."

That rooster sure sounds lucky to me, being a pet in New York. No wonder, showing that pet can help Ray to make new friends.

I love hearing these stories, almost as if… just by listening… I'm making new friends of my own. Whenever company comes for dinner, I really enjoy all those stories. But I'll admit, I'm getting tired of the other stories, stories that my parents use to teach me about life, especially when I don't feel like they're giving me the real answer at all.

For instance, why we don't belong to anything, the way that normal families do? Stories that are supposed to *explain everything*... don't. Instead, they remind me of those paintings made just for small children in my old bedroom at the last apartment, pictures like "The Dish & The Spoon," teaching me what children are supposed to learn about nursery rhymes, words repeated because other people have said them so often, words repeated over and over as if tradition makes them true.

No matter how often I would look at my bedroom wall and see that ridiculous imitation cow or the dish excitedly leaping away with the spoon, none of it ever made any sense to me. Except that grownups apparently need to repeat certain stories over and over and over. For example, around this time in my life (my too-long year of third grade) Mommy often tells this story. "I wanted to teach you about religion, I really did. But I couldn't. Blame the receptionist."

Following that, she explains, "I went to a synagogue to make arrangements for you to go to Sunday School and get a good Jewish education. This was very scary for me. I had terrible feelings of insecurity, but I want you to know that I did it anyway, because sometimes good mothers have to do difficult things. It's important that you appreciate how I always did my best for you.

"So there I was in the lobby of the synagogue. I was very vulnerable, trying to help you have more of a religion than I was given when I was your age! Very shy, but I tried to ask the receptionist, 'My daughter needs to have a religious education.'

"Well, this awful woman was busy, talking on the phone or something, even though I was standing right in front of her desk, and if she bothered to see my expression it would have been obvious to her how hard I was struggling to ask her this question.

"But did she do what was nice? Not at all. That selfish receptionist grabbed a piece of paper and shoved it over to me, very rudely, and then she told me, 'These are our rates.'

"Afterward she turned away, like I couldn't ask any other questions until I paid her. Mean and horrible!"

"Can you imagine? I ask about religion and all she tells me is, 'These are our rates'? What kind of religion is that? Luckily, I saw through the whole thing, and that's why you're never going to belong to any religion."

Guess this selfish, inconsiderate kind of talking happens a lot whenever my parents try to join things! Or maybe my parents stay home so much because my mother's a first-generation American and my father wasn't even born here, so they are still learning how to fit in.

However, they're not crying about it like a baby. They have become independent, which I can also do when I grow up. What matters, they tell me, is that they make their own fun.

Apart from Birdland and the guests at our home, Daddy hangs out with his War buddies, also with his old fraternity brothers from college. While Mommy always makes a best friend from the neighborhood. Then they can sit every day in each other's kitchens, discussing their problems while drinking coffee from cups that clink onto their saucers; drinking coffee, the grownup drink that smells bitter and brave. The Moms sip it and stir it and talk, talk, talk.

When my parents talk just to each other, I often manage to eavesdrop. What's their favorite topic? Psychological problems, especially the really awful ones that they call "neuroses." Whenever possible, I listen to grownup talk, squinting hard in my mind, trying to figure out what it all means. Lacking any big brother, I figure that eavesdropping on adult conversations is the best way that I can learn about life.

Plus, my parents get such a kick out of their stories about people, even if those stories don't make much sense to me. For example, Mr. and Mrs. Rosenbaum often chuckle about this one: how Daddy's good friend Irwin used to visit a lot and he'd come by subway, of course, carrying a book to keep him occupied. Eventually, my parents realized that it was always the same book, month after month.

How could they tell that Irwin's book always was the same? Because he'd made a book cover for it out of newspaper, and those stories from the New York Times never changed. Sure, people keep their books private sometimes. But the title of Irwin's book became a big mystery since, every visit, my parents would ask him, "So, what are you reading?"

Irwin kept telling them, "Nothing." The suspense was killing my parents, so they got sneaky. One visit, when Irwin went to the bathroom, Ernie and Sue ran over to see what kind of book was hidden beneath that mysterious paper cover. What was the title, already? *Sex without Guilt.*

Mommy and Daddy find this story hilarious. They tell that story to each other a lot. I guess they like it because it took them so many months before Irwin finally went to the bathroom when he was visiting them. Grownup things are often hard for me to understand, so I really, really wish that I had a big brother who could explain it all.

Another thing I'd like him to explain are the rules of our house. Because nobody else seems to live the way we do. Years later, I figure out those rules. Before ending this chapter, Questing Reader, I'll list them for you, just to round out my picture of where I spent my school years until college.

The Rosenbaum Family Rules

Like all parents, Ernie and Sue set up their home according to
what they believe. Being idealistic, they want to become better
parents than the ones they had. After putting serious thought into
it, they've figured out how to live in a totally modern way,
aiming to shape their daughters to become psychologically
healthy and free. So here are the rules of the house.

> - Instead of a bossy father, pushing everybody around, let
>   the children be free to make their own choices. Neither
>   nagging them to do their homework, nor ever giving
>   them advice about anything.
> - Instead of harsh rules and obligations, give their kids no
>   family chores whatsoever. Never force them to cook or
>   clean or earn money. They'll grow up soon enough.
> - Instead of horrible summer plans that led to misery
>   (Sue's history) or never having any vacations at all
>   (Ernie's childhood, so lacking in childhood), for
>   heaven's sake, let children be children, free to play and
>   make their own fun.
> - Instead of sexual prudery, with all of the hideous
>   behavior that "messed them up good," the Rosenbaum
>   daughters would live in a psychologically modern home,
>   free of inhibitions. Children should grow up in the
>   natural way, seeing their parents sleep naked, with open
>   bathroom doors and bedrooms, watching parents
>   confidently walk throughout the home completely
>   naked.
> - Instead of distant parents, pitiably out of touch with their
>   own neuroses, let Sue and Ernie's children hear the truth:
>   free discussions of their parents' emotional and sexual
>   histories; honest sharing about insecurities of all kinds.

Through unspoken family rules like these, home when I'm 8
years old is exactly how it will be when I'm 17, all because my

idealistic parents strive to give their kids a better upbringing than their own miserable childhoods.

Each of these beliefs seems fail-safe to them, downright liberating. Yet I will tell you this, Questing Reader. Decades later, when I become a parent in my own right, my husband and I will forcefully swing that discipline pendulum quite some distance from the extreme of those Rosenbaum Family Rules.

While I'm growing up, though, my parents keep doing their honest best to spare their children pain. Despite not succeeding as well as they wish, my parents do manage to make my childhood pretty darned happy, remarkably free, and always full of learning.

Seems to me… for a religion, a person could do a lot worse than "Find your own fun."

CHAPTER 12

There's a Place for Us

In fourth grade, I start a new school, the United Nations International School. My sister attends too, only I don't see her much because she's a baby in kindergarten.

Soon as my parents hear of this new school, they become very excited, especially my father. He does everything he can to get me accepted, and it works. A school like this costs lots of money, but he applied for scholarships for Amy and me, so that we can definitely go there. Telling me about this new school, Daddy's face shines the way it does whenever he's really, really excited about something. "You'll be with children from all over the world. Most of them have parents who work for the United Nations."

"U.N." is a nickname. Like that, the school has a nickname, too, "U.N.I.S." This pronounced "You-ness." I don't know any other school that has an initial for a nickname. This convinces me that my new school must be really important.

Every school day, Mommy drives Amy and me there, about three miles from home. At this fancy school they make us a hot lunch so that we don't have to walk home to eat sandwiches. My new school is in a bunch of garden apartments, like where our family lived before we moved to our big apartment in Flushing. Only what's different about this U.N.I.S. kind of place? Soon as you enter and start walking upstairs to the classroom, you go past a big kitchen with a funny kind of smell that I have never smelled before.

It's cooking for children, for a whole lot of children. Echoing smells tickle your nose whenever you walk by, like echoes from walking inside a long tunnel. Only these are smells from food that is cooked, then warmed over, then sits around some more. It fills the whole school, that day's smells, like mashed potatoes and canned green beans and beef. School meals don't have fun cooked into them, like the yummy, exciting casseroles that my mother cooks with tomato sauce and cheese and hamburger. Nor does it smell like the comforting meals at Grandma's, company food that is always hot roast beef and cold canned asparagus.

This school food is different, as if it clunks around in work boots. I guess that's how it must be with public food, made with regular ingredients on the outside, but not containing the inside part, that special seasoning I'm used to, called Love. For sure, the stomping smell of these meals lasts long after lunchtime. Even when it's time to go home after a long school day, when I walk past the closed-down kitchen, even then I can smell that funny smell.

At my new school, many other things are different. Classes are much more interesting than back at P.S. 164. Not so much fun for me, though, is how my teacher says I'm far behind at math and geography. Mommy says this proves that my old school wasn't so hot.

By the end of my first year, I've mostly caught up. Except for French: The sounds are hard, especially the strange gurgly way you're supposed to say R, where you're supposed to make a pool of spit in the back of your throat and then gargle with it, which is just plain disgusting. In class I'm always afraid that if I say that letter loudly in front of everybody, I will throw up.

Penmanship is hard, too. Mrs. Onychuk, my teacher for everything except French, is very proud of her strict ways with penmanship. Once she says, "If you always try your very best, soon it will become your ordinary." What a beautiful idea! I decide to try my best always, at everything. Unfortunately, for my handwriting practice, none of my trying seems to work. Teacher returns one of my first penmanship papers, complaining that it's too hard to read.

"How can I fix it?" I ask.

Teacher answers, "I can't tell you. Make the letters easier to read. Figure it out for yourself."

Sigh! All year long, I keep changing my writing, trying everything I can think of:

- ➢ Going from tiny little letters like baby teeth
- ➢ To tall, skinny letters like jail bars
- ➢ Concentrating hard to make sophisticated letters slanted toward the left
- ➢ Or offering up a way that's more eager-to-make-friends, where letters keep pushing hard to the right.
- ➢ Sometimes I'll offer up chubby letters that refuse to diet,
- ➢ While at other times, my skinny writing looks like spaghetti on a page.

And every one of these handwritings has the same purpose. I'm trying really hard to write well enough so that my teacher finally says, "Good job."

Some days, if I run out of ideas, I'll look at one of the other kids in my class. Then I'll feel how I'd write if I were that kid, which gives me a whole different way to clutch my fountain pen and go, go, go. Only no matter what, Teacher doesn't like that, either. Well, I keep trying to improve somehow, never writing the same way twice. Every penmanship class, I try my best and make up a completely new way to shape my letters. Maybe someday I will figure out which kind my teacher likes. Private school sure is different!

Recess is supposed to be more fun at the new school, because we go out to play in a huge vacant lot called "The baseball field." Not that I have any idea what a baseball is, or why it would need an entire field. What matters is that during recess we're supposed to run around and get fresh air. Only our group of ten girls is headed by two red-headed twins from England, Susan and Jennifer. They are very, very bossy. Since they don't like me, automatically that means none of the other kids is allowed to like me either.

I don't like all that not-liking, especially when we play tag. Once I'm "It," what happens if I try to tag somebody else? It's impossible, which makes no sense. But it's true.

Sometimes I feel as frustrated as when I was a helpless little baby and couldn't even roll over yet! By now I can walk and run, of course, but maybe not as fast as the others. Of course, I try my best, but while I'm running and panting, Susan and Jennifer secretly make faces at me behind my back (which I can tell because sometimes I'll quickly run in a new direction. Then I'll look over and see those mean faces).

Even if they didn't make fun of me, I'd feel bad enough, since every other girl in my class can run faster than me. When I get nearly close enough to tag someone, she'll escape by running faster than I can. Then the entire group has a nice, jolly laugh, a great big laugh, at me. Sometimes I'll spend my entire recess trying to tag somebody, anybody. But I never win, not once.

Would grownups just see happy children at play? Who knows? They're never around. If one came by and asked what we were doing, I'd say, "This game isn't only "Tag." Whatever these girls are playing, it hurts."

What's the best thing I manage to do with Tag? Not let the other kids see me cry. Instead, I make myself save it all up, like going to the bathroom. Soon as Mommy comes to pick me up after school, once I'm safe in the car, my face crumples up like a used Kleenex, and then out fall the tears.

I guess my mother thinks this is normal for kids, that I cry every school day. She is very understanding. In fact, one day, she even makes herself very vulnerable, telling me how she suffers so much that she's started going to a psychiatrist many days every week. This doctor helps her to recognize how sad she feels, and understand how all her pain began, so that she's making good progress now, although often she still feels very sad, and that's okay.

Because of therapy, Mommy has learned how to listen patiently while I let out my unhappy feelings. I can say anything, and that's okay. Questing Reader, I can tell my mother thinks that she would make a very good psychiatrist herself, some day.

Once back home, I have a big snack and then go do my homework. It's not much use telling either parent about my problems. You see, they're very nice, and they definitely care, but my stories remind them of all the troubles *they* had in childhood. Automatically they start telling me stories, really awful stories, about what happened to them.

True, this does take my mind away from my troubles. Still, it's not helping me to wind up in a happier place, more like visiting a really worse place which, sometimes, is downright scary. Not that my parents notice by then, since they're no longer looking at me but staring in that odd way people can have when they travel in their minds to someplace else. Their eyes remind me of the empty baseball field at school! Yet somehow, they manage to keep talking. Yes, for me, trying to get help from the parents is like going to a really worse place.

Eventually I figure out a plan. After I get home from school, I start writing stories. Soon I'm working on stories every day after school. I even name my first story. It's called *Jane's Plan*. Both words and pictures! The story is about a really nice girl named Jane who goes to a horrible school. The girls are very mean to her. She doesn't know what to do. Nobody helps her, not even her teacher or parents.

It would be nice if she had a big brother to help, but she doesn't. Nobody is there to help Jane. She must think of a plan on her own. After many days I finish writing this part of the story, but then I get stuck. You see, I don't really know what will come next. How discouraging, not being able to finish my story!

Still, I read the first part over and over. Somehow this comforts me. I do feel confident that someday I will finish Jane's story, and describe her excellent plan, and the story's ending will be happy. Of course, good things still happen in my life, every day, both outside of school and sometimes also while I'm in school. Because I really do love learning.

As a special treat, for my birthday, after school I go to The City. It's just my parents and me. Annoying little sister Amy has to stay at home with a babysitter, while my parents take me to see a new Broadway show that is supposed to be very good. It's called *West Side Story*.

Mommy especially loves Broadways shows. As a young woman she lived in The City where she would take beautiful walks in Central Park and go to Saturday matinees, with tickets so cheap they were almost free. Sue saw all the good shows in town. Her favorite was *South Pacific*, where Mary Martin would give herself a shampoo every time that she sang, *I'm Going to Wash that Man Right out of My Hair*.

The play we are going to see, *West Side Story*, is my first show ever. It is a musical, supposed to have the most exciting dances and beautiful songs. Once the big velvet curtain goes up, the feeling in the theater is like right before a thunder-and-lightning storm. Only the show doesn't go boom-and-flash and then nothing. Excitement stays switched on for the entire play. The song about *I Feel Pretty* reminds me of playing with dolls, like a fairyland.

A song called *There's a Place for Us* comes later. It makes me wonder, when I feel so lonely at school, is that because I'm in the wrong place? I wonder, does everybody have a right place, somehow, somewhere, some day? When I grow up, will there be somebody like Tony to hold my hand and take me to that right place at last?

My heart feels sore, as if it has been aching for a long time and I just noticed. Tears wet my cheeks. Those tears are icy cold. Daddy, sitting to my left, is weeping, too. His eyes are greenish hazel, like mine. How I look, mostly I take after my mother, except for having my father's eyes. His eyes are the same color as mine and they cry at the drop of a hat, just like mine.

Although *West Side Story* is a musical, there are some very sad parts. I did not know before that a musical could have sad parts. Gilbert and Sullivan operettas from England, long ago, are never so unhappy, not the ones I've heard, while this New York kind of musical definitely has some sad parts. While I'm thinking about all this, suddenly, a gun goes off and shoots Tony, the hero. Shoots him dead.

Never, I've never heard a gunshot before. Without meaning to, I scream full force. Then I burst into tears. Mommy comforts me, which of course, she's had plenty of practice at doing, between nursing me for the first five years of my life and now all my crying every day after school. Soon she's putting her arm around me, giving me a comforting squeeze, as usual, because my Mommy is always especially kind and patient whenever I feel unhappy.

Only this time, she looks embarrassed. So does Daddy. Gradually it dawns on me, how people in the audience are turning to look at me in a way that is not friendly, because this time I'm not wailing alone in the car with my mother. Instead, I'm sitting in the Winter Garden Theater and scream-crying because somebody just got killed. No other kids are around, at least none that I can hear. Nobody is crying along with me. Oh, how embarrassing!

Luckily people look away quickly, eager to get back to the show. Fast as I can, I make myself stop crying and get back, too. All of us want to find out what is going to happen to pretty Maria.

As Grandpa would ask, "What am I learning?"

Guess it would be this: Even bad feelings can go away, if you don't pay attention. I am learning to cover them up, like putting the lid on the garbage can in our kitchen. Or like wiping off the kitchen table with a rag, sweeping off all the crumbs. Easy! I like that kitchen table of ours. It happens to be colored a bright yellow.

CHAPTER 13

Flying as Best I Can

"History is just one damned thing after another." This is Mr. Sullivan's favorite quote, which might seem odd since he is a history teacher. I've had him as my history teacher ever since sixth grade. Now I'm in eighth grade, and this man still doesn't think history means a damned thing, plus his voice still contains no music in it, never has, as if the man talks in all consonants and doesn't believe that vowels even exist.

Mr. Sullivan is the kind of person who makes you shake your head and sigh; after two years, he's still telling us that same quote and, to him, it's the most hilarious joke in all the world. Every time.

It's 1962, which means I am 14 years old. My sarcasm has been developing nicely; I only wish that my bust development would keep pace; I wish a lot of things. A different history teacher would be nice, for instance. At least I have two other teachers whom I do like.

Mademoiselle Jané has been my French teacher for more than two years now, and besides packing conjugations into my brain, she manages to open a certain kind of door inside my head, the door to learning languages. While we're in class, she speaks French and mixes it up with English. This has tricked me until I've stopped worrying about whether French sounds are disgusting. By now I just understand what she's saying.

Coming from Cuba, Mademoiselle Jané could teach Spanish but we're supposed to learn French from her. She's slim, with dark skin and quick brown eyes, plus a mouth that somehow moves livelier than other people's mouths.

But my very favorite person at school — heck, my favorite grownup besides my Dad — is Monica Lacrouts, now my English teacher for the second year in a row. She's the only teacher I've met in all my years at U.N.I.S who seems to like me and think I am smart.

Granted, Mrs. Lacrouts isn't the prettiest teacher, with straight blonde hair that seems allergic to style, and piercing blue eyes in the palest of blues. Also, her stout body seems to contain more skin than other people wear on their bodies, maybe due to a skin color that is ultra-pale and loaded with freckles. Or maybe she seems to have extra skin because of only wearing one kind of shoe, moccasins, moccasins worn with no stockings.

How can a grownup be woman allowed to do that? Even I wear stockings for special occasions, complete with a weird garter belt that you've got to use to prevent stockings from falling off, and especially weird are the rubbery stocking holders like buttons that dangle down from the garter belt. Some women wear a similar contraption to fasten their sanitary napkins, but my mother has taught me to use tampons; she says that's the only good way, the modern way.

Every woman has a story of when she first got her period, and I suppose mine is no stranger than most. One morning before school, sitting on the toilet, I notice blood on my underpants. So, I run to wake up my mother. Already we'd had The Conversation. Now all I have to do is wake Mom up, which requires me to yell "Mommy, Mommy" like a kid, right by her ear. Then I explain several times that today is the day and finally

I have It, eventually whispering an awkward word I have never said out loud before: "Menstruating."

Once I finally drag my mother into a seated position, she knows exactly what to do. First, rummaging around, she finds a box of tampons and shoves it into my hands; next Mom removes one of these strange tampons from the box and tells me to unwrap it.

Helping like this is about all she can handle. From this point onward, Mom insists on coaching me from outside the bathroom door; keeping it closed for once, which is odd in my apartment, usually home to the Proudly Naked Parents. Through that closed door, Mom starts explaining what to do with the tampon. Her upset voice alternates between brisk instructions and longer explanations…. Versus talking about the topic of greater importance to her: how having this conversation is very traumatic for her, not my fault; but having to deal with a daughter under these circumstances is a very disturbing reminder of her own terrible, anguish-filled history with menstruation.

After the first ten minutes or so, Mom starts telling me just one thing: "Push." Sue keeps saying, "Push." There I am, struggling to get that huge tampon (still in its big carboard holder) into a place that I hadn't really known existed within my own body, because now this isn't just an idea from my one Facts of Life conversation but rather a newly discovered part of my physique, and a part that's slippery right now in a way I don't want to think about, let alone touch.

Making my job even more confusing, the enormous tampon doesn't want to go all the way in, apparently, and I sure can't risk going to school with a falling-out Tampax. So I stick up for myself, even though Mom clearly wants to get all this over with and go back to a deeply snoring sleep. I insist that she keep telling me what to do until this weird new job is done.

Our conversation grows ever-louder and faster, with Mom eventually urging me in her strictest voice, "Push harder. Your tampon must go in completely." Finally, one last shove does it; one pop and then the thing is in me at last; and now I am officially a woman, a woman who knows how to handle a tampon.

Sue goes back to bed, probably to cry over her big ordeal as a mother. Years later, it occurs to me that the popping sensation I've felt means that I just lost my hymen. Oh well.

Back to the topic of school, where lots of us girls are women now, U.N.I.S. has moved to a different building, moving all the way from Parkway Village in Queens to a great big building in Manhattan. This tall schoolhouse, on 70th Street and First Avenue, was built during the Civil War. For some reason, it was later abandoned by the public schools. This made it possible for my school to snap it up like a big, tall bargain. Really, they couldn't have found a place that would be more fun for a student like me.

Windows here are gigantic; ultra-long windows that open with ultra-long wooden poles; each window pole built with a bizarre T-shaped pusher piece at the end. What kid wouldn't love these ancient contraptions? Or the rest of this crazy place! Hallways are so high, they echo; and every staircase contains so many steps, connecting each of the four enormous stories.

I wonder, how did this amazing place happen? Back when this place was built, were all children taller, built more like Abe Lincoln? Or were the kids normal-sized, but wearing those tall black hats? What else could explain building each floor so high, with ceilings like a cathedral? Anyhow, I love all the exercise. Running up and down all day, sprinting from one classroom to another, so many steps all day long; it's making my legs really strong. Best of all, this building isn't just echoey and ancient and tall. It contains secret places.

Amazingly, by now I have a best friend who joins me in exploring these places. Yes, Questing Reader, finally I have a best friend! Her name is Joyce Green. She has exactly the same birthday as me, and we might be twins except that she is a Negro and I am white. Joyce has a beautiful voice for singing; she's pretty and funny and sweet, and we always find so much to talk about. Once I even got to sleep over at her house and we played with her pet, a tiny kitten, the first cat I've ever seen in my life.

At school we've discovered a special place that's almost like an amusement park. Here's how we find it. One lunch break, Joyce and I are doing our usual exploration of the immense school building when we discover something most peculiar. Imagine, Questing Reader, there's a back hallway on the ground floor where the staircase ends suddenly, dropping away into nothing. And guess what else? Back in the old days they must have had so much room that they just sprinkled extra spaces around, like ketchup to go with your French fries.

Because this staircase ends with some extra space in the back, that leaves a space that's totally empty. Basically, the staircase stops short, with a big wide space circling all around it. Even better, an old-fashioned pole is attached four steps up from the bottom of that staircase. Imagine, a 10-foot-tall pole that attaches to nothing at all but the bottom of a staircase, with so much extra room on all sides. Why build that?

Why? Wow! Because right in the same split-second, Joyce and I figure out how we can take turns flying around, using that pole. To start, you stand on the fifth step from the bottom and then, grabbing that pole tightly with both hands, you leap off, swinging both legs out to the side.

As you twirl around, momentum builds through most of a full circle, until you feel like you're flying. Finally, you let go of the pole and fall onto the floor, giggling. During that leap, it feels as though you've taken a ride all the way out into space and gone weightless. Every day we can, Joyce and I wolf down our lunches, then dash over to our special, secret place, taking turns. Because every time that we twirl into weightlessness, it feels just like flying.

All the rest of our time together, we're talk like crazy. Yes, we talk about *everything*. So much goes on every day at U.N.I.S., especially obvious to us since we're teenagers now. It's so important to have a friend who understands what matters, like:

> ➤ Why do our teachers act the way that they do?
> ➤ All the homework we're supposed to do. (Complaining about homework becomes our art form.)
> ➤ How are the other kids treating us?
> ➤ Praising everything we like. Criticizing in great detail every single thing that bothers us.
> ➤ Most of all, trying to figure out, how will things change when we finally grow up?

Such a relief, having a best friend at last!

CHAPTER 14

Teenage Discoveries

Now that I've reached the age of 15, food has turned jumbo delicious. Especially since I've invented the yummiest recipe, Marble Toast, which transforms our usual Wonder Bread into a wonderland of sophistication.

Questing Reader, would you like to learn how to make it? You start with crisp toast, still hot. Slather it with crunchy peanut butter, at least half an inch thick. Artistically plop down several tablespoons of the most delectable jelly — let's face it, "most delectable" means *any* flavor of jelly — and then you can use the tip of a knife to draw swirls. Soon the two main colors blend into a Jackson Pollock-style masterpiece, something truly unique in the world, lovely to admire for a few long seconds as you hold it there on your hand (because who needs to bother with a plate?) and always this food creation looks uniquely fascinating. Yet compared to how it tastes, the sight of it is *nothing*.

Once a bite of gooey, delectable Marble Toast enters my mouth it sings, sings louder, squeaks with joy, cutely yells "Gobble, gobble, gobble," and soon makes me groan with pleasure, almost as if my tongue is applauding. Afterward a chorus of taste buds sings "More, more, more." Until, with great regret, after several slices, I admit that I'm full.

Oh, life is good when I'm 15 years old. I'd be called a sophomore if I went to public school, like my first-floor neighbor Karen, who goes to Jamaica High, or if I went to

Catholic High School, like my friend Maureen. At U.N.I.S. they call it "Tutorial One" in that funny way they have, bending over backward to not favor Americans — when our school is supposed to be international but most of the kids come from where? New York, just like me.

Ridiculous but loveable, that's school to me now, something you're stuck with, like family; my ridiculous private school, with our "biggest ever" class that I'm in, practically miniscule, since we've got just 16 kids. And only 5 of them are boys.

Younger grades, like Amy's, are bigger; but still it's such a teensy, tiny school in that immense, antiquated building, with us kids running around like ants at a picnic for giants; giants being the kind of people for whom those weird high ceilings were originally built (I've decided by now). With no warning, my friend Joyce has disappeared from U.N.I.S. She got accepted at Performing Arts, a big magnet school in the city, and never even said goodbye, which I cried about for a while, but what can you do?

Now I'm friendly with Shoba from India, whose Dad works at the U.N.; and Danuta from Poland, whose Dad is an economist; and Donna, whose father comes from Barbados I think, and he must do something. What's the best thing about Donna? I love how she got into trouble the first time she wrote an essay for Mrs. Lacrouts. "You couldn't possibly have written that all by yourself," said Mrs. Lacrouts.

But Donna did, she sure did. It's such fun being friends with an adolescent who already thinks like a grownup. And speaking of grownups, I've started to meet older kids at school. Maybe I have a little crush on Mark Zorn, so sophisticated; along with his baby brother John, who is going to be a musician. (Three renowned composers are part of my U.N.I.S life, actually: both

John Zorn; Steven Hartke, my sister's first boyfriend; and my simpatico Spanish teacher, Leonardo Balada.)

Thanks to Mark, I discover Jean Shepherd's radio show. He tells stories that are realer than real, as a radio hero who isn't afraid of anything. Every show he'll get to a "That's life" part of his story and then he'll play his kazoo in a carefree (yet Nyah, Nyah) kind of way. Mr. Shepherd is the most dazzlingly sophisticated person I've ever met, perfect for helping me to learn about becoming a grownup. Though I haven't met the great storyteller in person, I do own one of the new transistor radios, so it feels like he's a real person in my life. Especially enjoyable is how sneak-listen to him under the covers, after I turn out the lights at bedtime, like I'm supposed to do.

Besides Mark, another older kid at school is Gita from India, mysteriously graceful, slim and elegant. In her purse she keeps a little tin of breath mints, but when she opens it up to show me, what's inside? All the regular mints are gone. Instead that tin is full of a twig-like kind of spice, "cloves." Gita reaches for one and hands it to me. "Just put this in your mouth and chew it," she says, offering me a chance. I try my clove and find it good, not sweet but fascinating; whenever I chew, out pop layers and layers of deep earth flavor.

Otherwise, my favorite snack is the violet-perfumed chewing gum that Shoba and I buy at the candy store. Now that's flavor!

By now I've got many lives within my one life, just like different foods you could put on a shiny TV dinner tray. I've got the school life, full of drama; my family life, which I'm still not crazy about, but that's supposed to be normal for an adolescent; and all my friends from the neighborhood. Most of the school kids are rich, living either in Manhattan or Parkway Village. While my neighborhood buddies are more like me, not snobby about their clothes, never going to dermatologists or orthodontists; and definitely never bragging about going on Home Leave, all paid for by the U.N.

In 1963, autumn is my favorite season. In my part of Flushing, Queens, nature is no big deal, and yet we do have one immense oak tree where 78th Avenue meets Main Street. Besides that we've got smaller trees too. All the fallen leaves litter the sidewalk with the most astonishing colors, like fighting orange, regal yellow, and resigned-but-calm-ish brown.

Even better, autumn brings smells that you never find at other times of the year, sorrowful earthy odors of moldering complication. One day that I will never forget, my autumn turns magical. This happens when I'm walking back home, giving no thought to moldering complication (at least, outside of my intriguing inner life as a teenage girl) when, bam! I see that the stately oak has thrown down all its leaves. And I mean all of them, Questing Reader.

Heaps of fragrant leaves are so plentiful that I start kicking them into one gigantic pile, then take a running leap and smash myself way down onto that pile. Again and again, I create a small hill of leaves, then roll around in them, transforming away. That's the kind of game I could play forever, with every second a thrill.

Autumn is also a season of longing, and doesn't teenage me know a lot about that! Evenings, I'm drawn to my bedroom window. Losing track of time I'll gaze dreamily at the black sky, any star serving as a wishing star, so that I can ask God to help me grow up at last.

Admittedly I also have a more specialized longing: whenever leaning out my window, maybe this time I might be lucky enough to see Jimmy Lovelace. Jimmy is my age, big and tall, so handsome, with his blond hair and muscular build. Sure, we've talked sometimes, probably because he has a crush on my friend Annette, like many guys around here. Probably, Jimmy feels longing a lot like mine, only it's for Annette. Still, at my window I'm free to dream of Jimmy, trying hard to spot him out there in the dark, since several times a day he goes out walking his big poodle Puddin'. How can I help him to notice me?

All I can think of is this: Look for him out my window, wishing fervently that he will see me somehow, really see me for the first time, at last. Then my life might turn into Romeo and Juliet, or Tony and Maria from *West Side Story* (but without the loud gunshot).

Oh, gunshots really do happen in the world. Here's how I find out. One day I'm playing in the back yard at Danuta's after school. Briskly, her mother walks outside, looks at me, and says flatly, "Your President Kennedy was just shot."

How could that be? Noble President Kennedy, who fights with the prejudiced man at the schoolhouse door in the South, that ugly Governor Wallace I've seen on TV. My smart president is a hero, like Dr. Martin Luther King. How can my president be gone, just like that?

Kennedy is the first American president I've grown to love, ever since I heard his speech where he asked everybody watching to ask inside themselves how they could help our country, and not just expect him to fix everything. Like so many kids, probably, when I heard Kennedy say those words, I told him and God, "Yes, I will find a way to help. I promise." Now, Kennedy shot? What kind of a world is this, anyway?

But then seasons go on and, like all Americans (plus my international friends from school, like Danuta), I go on living too. It helps that winter comes, because winter just might be my favorite season. Partly because of the Christmas presents but also because of the snow.

Drifts pile up near the garage area on my block, piling up in such a way that we kids can do the most thrilling athletic jumps ever, our invented wintertime sport for kids, only to be found on 78th Avenue, Flushing, Queens. Questing Reader, here's how we do it. In one place that grownups must not know about, beneath the sidewalk, there's an extra layer of space lower down. Cars can park there, this space is so big, and it fits together with the sidewalk in a weird way. Guess that's because my side of the block is higher than the other side.

Here's what matters: On the high side of my block, a big snowdrift always forms under that certain part of the sidewalk, creating a pile of snow even taller than me. We kids have discovered a perfect place for jumping into that snow. We line up quietly and then, when it's your turn, you leap off the pavement into that fluffy white snowdrift.

Probably all the kids love this jumping ritual, love it as much as I do, but we never discuss this out loud. We line up almost reverently, unusually quiet. Even the bossiest kids are willing to take their turn, totally willing to wait; anticipating this unique thrill, our hearts racing. And I guess you could say that we're chilled by the bitter cold but equally warmed by the crazy adventure of what we're about to do.

When my turn comes, first I leap upward as high as I can, adding to the drama of my big drop downward. Falling through space like a swooping bird, falling gloriously, soon I am welcomed back to earth and hugged by a fluffy white snowdrift. Snow jumping like this gives a stronger feeling of flying, even, than playing Twirl the Pole with Joyce at U.N.I.S.

> ➢ Or running around outside in small circles, tilting inward as far as I can without falling.
> ➢ Or holding out my arms and twirling, like a whirling dervish (whatever that's supposed to mean), until the

most delightful dizziness makes me fall down and giggle.

Best of all is when I can jump into a huge snowdrift and, for one sweet moment, feel exactly how a bird must feel, free to fly at will. Afterward, of course, you have to get up fast, so the next kid can go. And as you walk away, maybe you realize that a bunch of snow has gone up your nose. But who cares?

Leaps like that are just one of a zillion games that we teenagers make up this year, one-of-a-kind games that we invent for playing in the snow. Going back to school after winter break seems like a creative letdown. Except it's pretty consoling that Roger, a handsome new boy in my class, is ordered to sit next to me, sharing the other half of my wooden double-desk.

Naturally I can hardly pay attention to a word teachers say since, for the first time, I'm sitting really close to a teenage boy; inches away from him, really; and it's so confusing, trying to peek at Roger (and, especially, smell him) yet also appear to not be the least bit interested. Roger is a friendly guy, with a free-sounding way of pronouncing his words. Right away he becomes popular. What's really shocking about him, though?

Since Roger just came here from Australia, he's been having summer. Whenever he mentions this, casual-like, wow! That idea of Us-Winter versus Roger-Summer… it twirls my inner world more than any spinning geography globe.

Meanwhile, I find a different way to make my life more adventurous. This happens on New Year's Eve, when I decide it's high time that I stayed up all night, finally, up all night for my first time ever. So downstairs neighbor, Karen, and hatch a plan. Here's how we carry it out, Questing Reader.

While everyone else is asleep, we sneak outside and meet downstairs in front of our building; it's around 2:00 in the morning. Inspired by the enormous black sky, we talk. There's just enough moon to reveal a huge set of stars (many more than I've ever seen while keeping vigil for Jimmy).

Speaking in hushed voices, which seems only right as we boldly stand there in the dark, we're two independent girls beneath the vast sky. And our words are framed by a new kind of quiet. This happens because we're hearing no traffic noise at all, for a change; and underlying every word that we speak is a new kind of discovery. You see, there is nothing, nothing bigger than all the night sky.

Soon we drift into remembering a shared mystery long forgotten, as if girls like us have stood beneath this very same sky for as long as people have lived on earth: girls living in lonely farms or in cities teeming with noise from too many people; sometimes waiting for sailing ships to return, other times stuck in a landlocked life as predictable as the lowing of cattle... people trapped in their lives except for special moments like we're having right now, when we remember how free we are to look upward like this. Yes, free.

Even cavemen who could barely think, they must have seen it, that sky; and tribal people bossed around by their village chiefs; even shackled slaves who might briefly feel freed simply because the sky was so vast, and for a few moments their eyes could own a rich emptiness that they had a right to see, just like anyone else. Because every one of earth's people who felt small, eventually they must have discovered how they could look upward. And maybe that simple black sky might have whispered to them the very same thing we are feeling now, "Never give up hope."

That's how I am feeling, anyway, safe in the blackness, as if it's promising me that somehow life could be more, more, more. As Karen and I stand there in the dark, we're far too thrilled to feel sleepy. In fact, it's as if we start waking up from the dream of our teenage lives here in Queens. And so we begin to talk, really talk.

During pauses in our conversation, I wonder, how even the most powerful of men, and even the most arrogant of women — how each human alive might sometimes feel the need to look for something bigger, inspired by standing beneath that enormous night sky.

And that would always be possible, no matter what. Then the sight of that night sky could supply you with a bigger kind of knowing, a kind of peace that was missing before. Bringing exactly whichever thoughts or feelings you needed most to complete you; whatever might complete you for one unforgettable moment, or maybe even longer.

Somehow our familiar-but-dull brick courtyard becomes a place of great expectations. Beneath the stars as we've never seen them before, Karen and I discover a special kind of conversation, growing close to each other in an adult way that I've never had with anyone else so far, talking as if *only truth can be spoken here*, beneath this all-knowing sky.

For the very first time, out loud, we admit to each other (and maybe ourselves) how, more than anything else, we're so curious about what life could be; how secretly, whenever no grownup is looking, we're busily trying to figure out what life could mean.

As we keep talking, Karen's familiar face begins to look different to me. For the first time, I see the unusual shade of her light brown eyes, and also the adorable way that her curvy eyebrows twist around whenever she's thinking hard. Soon I see something else that's surprising. Both of us notice it the same instant, with a jolt. Toward the end of the night, quite mysteriously, shapes begin to form out of indigo light.

Following that, this palest of pastel lights begins to paint everything else with color.

Soon those half-seen shapes of things are going to become familiar objects, like the most popular bench in our courtyard, where for years I've watched the gossipy mothers. Only now it's as though every single thing in this courtyard has been created completely new, created in honor of this brand new day, created just for Karen and me.

Then the milkman interrupts us because he comes carrying his glass bottles. Long before seeing him, we hear the clinking of the glass. That small tinkling sound startles Karen and me. Instantly we're transported back into our everyday neighborhood.

For sure, the milkman sees us now, so he must know that we're not supposed to be up all night. Karen and I swap glances, feeling a little guilty because usually we're good girls but this time we really did sneak out and stay up all night. Probably the milkman won't tell our parents. Even so, our night-to-dawn magic is broken. After a quick goodbye, we run back into our apartments and don't speak another word to each other about all this specialness. Not ever.

But, Questing Reader, afterward I might begin to appreciate colors a bit more. That spring is when I start to notice how plant colors appear in May, surprising as those impossibly fresh colors of dawn, but these spring colors must secretly grow inside certain plants, because all of a sudden they show themselves as if coming out from nowhere.

For example, I'm used to walking past twiggy hedges outside my apartment courtyard, unimpressive plants that I usually pass without taking a second look. Yet this spring I catch how they brighten up and bloom, impossible as a rabbit being pulled out of a hat, the kind of magician's act that I'm used to watching on

TV, like *The Ed Sullivan Show*. Only what we get here is far better than some squirmy bunny caught in front of a camera.

Overnight there's been a change to our wintertime hedges. *Forsythia* they're called, and usually I think of them as ugly and stiff, trimmed severely with flat tops, hedges that don't seem like living things because they've been shaped into walls. Only this spring, all of a sudden, every single branch starts growing soft new blossoms. Guess those wall-like plants were really alive all along, now turning a sudden shade of yellow, as startling as if each tiny blossom was boldly painted with the essence of spring.

Noticing this makes me so glad. Isn't spring everybody's favorite season? Spring is definitely my favorite season. And this year, to make springtime even more special, somebody has organized a kind of benefit fundraiser for our nonprofit U.N. International School. Although I don't understand exactly how the fundraiser part works, I do know this. All of us kids get to dress up and go to the ballet, seeing Rudolf Nureyev dance with Margot Fonteyn. They're very famous dancers right now.

So their performance is supposed to be gorgeous and artistic. This is a little embarrassing to admit, but I don't get the point. After the ballet is over, my class sits in a fancy room filled with big, round tables that have fresh flowers for decoration. Then all of us get to eat banquet-style food -- all good looks but hardly any flavor.

Here's the most special part. We're given champagne. Naughty, naughty! I drink a whole glass, which makes me tipsy for the first time in my life. How do I celebrate? By eating one of the carnations on our floral centerpiece, a pink one.

After this amazing springtime, filled with exciting discoveries, summer comes; surprising everybody, I guess. At least this summer surprises everyone who's capable of wonder. And do you know what summer means now, Questing Reader? What's different this summer, now that I'm nearly all grown up?

Until school starts in September I'm allowed to play outdoors, without asking permission, staying outdoors every night for as long as I like. It's the strangest thing, how I'd forgotten this. But summer has always been my favorite season. Playing all day with the other kids, running beneath the sprinklers at a nearby playground — what could be more fun than that?

No matter which time of year it is, or which group of kids I'm with, I do seem to be growing up okay. Somehow. Despite still not knowing how to grow up, not really. Every single year, life is getting better for me, a life that is turning out to be pretty darned good.

CHAPTER 15

Fear like a Forest Fire

This year two different girls invite me to their Sweet Sixteen parties. Cheryl Constan's bash includes boys. One of them gives me a parting kiss on the lips right before I go home, softly kissing me as if he's respectful but interested. Although I don't even know his name, technically this does count as my first kiss, at last! This boy is a tall guy, with coffee-colored skin and eyes the color of Tootsie Rolls.

The other party is for a different classmate at U.N.I.S., Fritzi Feist. As the highlight of the party, we don't play childish games like at a little kid's party, nor do we play the kissing game called "Spin the Bottle." Instead Fritzi's mother plays Reporter, with a real, live microphone that she holds while interviewing all of us party guests, sitting in a circle on her soft, red, living room rug.

Fritzi's Reporter Mom isn't just playing. She's Lisa Howard, a reporter on ABC, and America's first TV anchorwoman. Her daughter Fritzi would be easy to envy. She's pretty, with the figure of a very grownup — and very curvy — woman, and Fritzi is really bright, and not just academically. She seems street-smart beyond her years.

Lisa Howard will become even more famous, years later, for her suicide. But that's going to be Fritzi's trauma, not mine, worthy of many memoirs about her life, including the story of her larger-than-life mother. In this memoir of mine, Questing Reader, I'll tell you about three relatively major happenings from my life in 1964: three traumas, and then something unexpectedly wonderful.

By the time I'm 16, Amy and I get along much better. I admire her pretty hair, with its big bold curls, shiny and black. Her eyes are deep shade of brown, just like Mom's, but their mouths are very different. Since Amy's mouth holds no sarcasm. Hers is a gentle, young mouth that combines short and shy and expressive.

My sister is smart alright, and far more musical than I'll ever be. Most impressive of all is Amy's sense of smell, how she notices things I never would, like the time when we come home from a family visit and she observes matter-of-factly, "Aunt Carol's apartment smells exactly the same as it did the last time we visited, two years ago."

What if I ask for specifics? Then Amy can toss out a quick list of nose-details like it's nothing. Regarding my favorite aunt's house, it smells of "At least five kinds of perfume, lemon furniture polish, a lot of tears, and wine." Never bragging about being talented, that's my sweet sister. Mm modest sister expects that everybody else can do her special somethings.

I'm especially grateful to have Amy with me when the family packs into our car and we go to visit relatives. Always the driver is Mom, who often has panic attacks these days. She insists on being the driver because that "calms her down." Dad will sit next to her, talking extra-calmly, like The Most Reasonable Person in the World. He talks more and more calmly, intensely calmly, while Mom mutters things like, "I'm going to crack up."

Dad always knows what to say, like "No, you won't." And "Kids, we're getting close to the Wrigley Gum factory. Be sure to smell the Black Jack." Ernie has figured out how to handle Sue and her panic attacks, but these family drives feel like having the Cuban Missile Crisis right in our car, or an air raid drill like the kind at school where you hide under your desk to escape atom bombs.

Stuck-stuck-stuck in the back seat of the car, that's Amy and me. Meanwhile, Mom the Driver describes her fears in thrilling detail. She chain smokes. She cries and gasps. Yet, somehow, Sue Rosenbaum always manages to use her turn signal perfectly.

In theory, both of Sue's daughters know that we're supposed to feel sorry for her. Only by now, we've grown so weary of Mom and her phobias. Whenever she starts to use her scared voice, it makes me feel sick to my stomach. Stuck in the car like, forever, Amy and I will look at each other and make faces. This helps a little.

Mom's problems are small, though, compared to those of her sisters. For example, my sophisticated Aunt Carol apparently has some big problems. To get a sense of how special she is, Questing Reader, you might want to know that she's a big admirer of the popular actress Bette Davis. This, I'm told, explains why my aunt is glamorously bitter, and somehow larger than life. A chain smoker like my parents, Aunt Carol holds her cigarettes with exceptional flair, using plenty of flirtatious wrist action. And she cooks delicious meals with red wine in the gravy.

But back when Carol was married, her husband Bernie didn't appreciate her cooking. Once, in the middle of dinner, Mom told us, he flew into a temper tantrum. Then he picked up the pot roast from the serving dish and threw it at her. After that, she had to get a divorce. Now my Mom's older sister lives in a tiny apartment in The City along with my Cousin Jay, sometimes. (Other times, Jay lives with his father instead.)

Much as I love my Aunt Carol, I'm told that she has a drinking problem. For instance, she keeps getting fired from her work as a secretary. At least she doesn't let that bother her! Knowing the family secret about her drinking scares me a little. I hate the idea that a person could lose control in life, whether it's Aunt Carol drinking, or Mom with her phobias, or what happens when Dad comes home from work and he stands in front of the ice box, shoving food into his mouth, because he can't help it. What could be scarier?

Well, on this day I learn there can be more severe mental illness. The scene goes down like this. There we are, at Aunt Elly's apartment, visiting on a Sunday afternoon. Aunt Carol plus all four of us Rosenbaums, together we're having a stiff but pleasant conversation, when all of a sudden -- and I mean out of nowhere -- Aunt Elly begins to cry and scream.

Oh yes, I do mean *scream!*

She won't calm down, either, no matter how the other grownups plead with her, "Please calm down." Nothing works. Soon her big voice yells so loudly you can hear it out the windows and down onto the street below. I'm embarrassed to think how total strangers on the block and beyond... can hear and feel my aunt having a breakdown.

Such a big voice Aunt Elly has: Once upon a time, she proudly sang in the chorus at the Metropolitan Opera. Now this relative of mine is yelling in a way that is exactly the opposite of proud. So scary, what's happening during this visit; it reminds me of a forest fire that spreads out of control, turning the bright green trees into a scary red orange, reminding me of the TV commercial where Smoky the Bear says "Only you can prevent forest fires."

But who can prevent this family kind of a fire? In Aunt Elly's living room it feels like the craziness spreads from Aunt Elly to

Aunt Carol to Mom and then back to Aunt Elly again, while my Dad keeps trying to put that fire out, but the smoke never goes away, and maybe the flames burn him just a bit too. When I grow up, I would like to prevent forest fires, if only I can find out how.

Half an hour later, all of us guests flee the apartment. Aunt Elly has asked us to leave. Several weeks later Mom mentions in passing that, eventually, my aunt recovered, whatever that means. Maybe Elly had one to stay in a mental hospital. Or maybe, somehow, she fixed herself up on her own.

Mom doesn't like to talk about Elly, saying that she wants to protect Amy and me from hearing too many details. But she can't protect me from my next big trauma, which involves her and my Dad, and happens a few months later, when — like Cheryl and Fritzi — I turn sixteen. Warning: You're going to read about a trauma.

Incidentally, how can I tell what counts as a trauma? Despite hearing Mom talk about her traumas so much, the word has always seemed vague to me. But now, thanks to Aunt Elly, I have found a working definition: Trauma happens when time stops and everything feels extra vivid, and you feel like your soul is being singed… until you can almost smell the burning.

On the rare occasions when I've tried to press my clothes, using one of those heavy, electric clothes irons, I'll admit it, sometimes I've made a burning smell like that on a shirt. It's hard to be perfect, trying to do grownup things; and apparently I'm not the only one in my family who struggles with imperfection, which brings me next to the second trauma on my little list.

CHAPTER 16

Naked Misery

The night of my second trauma begins with a happy smell of home cooking. It's Sunday, a bowling night for my parents. Whenever they go out to play with their bowling league, I win every time, because I'm left at home, all alone except for my sister. She takes such good care of herself, it's as if she isn't even there. So I'm free to do whatever I want, which often means trying to cook.

Some nights find me making White Pull Candy, following a recipe in *The Joy of Cooking*, a candy of near-mythical status for this emerging confectioner. If made right, will it taste of unicorns and fairies?

Sadly, I'll never know: given that my homemade candy never comes out the same way twice, unless you simply call each attempt a "failure." In the back of my mind, I realize that some of this failure may be due to lacking what's called a "candy thermometer," which is referred to in my cookbook as being essential if you plan to make candy. However, my Mom doesn't have one. Besides, the very idea of this kind of thermometer seems weird to me. At my house there's just one way to take a temperature, and that stick-like thing with a bulb on the end is meant to be used *rectally*.

So ick! How can that possibly apply to cooking food in a saucepan? Turning up my nose at silly thermometers, what happens every time that I try making this lovely confection? My reward is a bizarre mess, solid and lumpen, inedible unless my incisors could develop the strength of jackhammers. Alas, making this candy is quite consistent with my other pursuits to express teenage longing. One way or another, it feels like I'm constantly stirring and yearning.

Although I'm not disappointed at the inevitable failures, not exactly. When things don't work out, I feel an inescapable nostalgia for what might have been, then console myself by replaying in my imagination what I yearned to make happen. Such as? Such as the fun of tugging on that delicious pull candy; maybe inviting Amy into the kitchen so that we can sprinkle on gorgeous food coloring, giggling with delight. And then, of course, we would feast away.

My other cooking experiments on bowling nights involve potatoes, which you might well think of as a solid and dependable sort of food. Well, maybe, not so dependable, considering how much I know so far about cooking. Nonetheless, this is my second favorite culinary specialty: not whimsical candy but down-to-earth, totally delicious, pan-fried potatoes; a delicacy that I've never actually tasted, and yet I can imagine it vividly enough, as if this has been my favorite food in some recent incarnation.

Instagram-imagine it for yourself, Questing Reader: the image of a hearty, German-style, potato dish, where each crispy bite delivers a meltingly gorgeous, soft-spudly goodness, and yet every piece also looks perfectly well-browned on the outside, crunchy in a way that simply never happens when Mom heats up frozen Potato Puffs.

Unfortunately, Mom has refused to teach me to cook; apparently this would stir up too many memories of her own childhood sorrows, reminding her of countless cruelties from her wicked stepmother. So once again, I'm on my own when it comes to potato cookery, exploring away. This particular Sunday night,

I'm sweating over the stove, hoping that somehow a great potato dish will come together, which would mean that I really can cook – that is, cook something besides Marble Toast.

Yes, me! A self-taught cook, downright spunky… and maybe, as of tonight, especially good at potato cookery. Only that doesn't happen. Years later, I'll get a clue why. About preparing those potatoes? Before pan-frying them, it's better to have already cooked the potatoes until soft. Failure is pretty much guaranteed if you use big raw chunks, such as those I've just sliced and thrown into the skillet.

Quickly, my cooking produces results, as dreams meet reality right there in my frying pan. Yet again, I'm shocked, shocked! Not one of my greasy, sad, little chunks of potato is edible, neither the singed surfaces nor the raw innards. There's really not much for taste buds to enjoy. (Not that this stops me from sampling many mouthfuls, ever hopeful.)

Eventually, I slink back to my bedroom, playing my favorite record on the record player. It's *La Boehme*, where struggling artists Mimi and Rudolpho fall in love, and he sings about her beautiful cold little hand, building up to their supremely romantic duet that usually moves me to tears, and does, that night; my romantic kind of weeping wells up from my hungering heart to the weird burnt taste in my mouth, while a small prayer to God slips into my mind. Couldn't I please, please find some boy to love me?

Then it's off to toothpaste time and staring at my pimples in the bathroom mirror, followed by the fitful first hour or so of insomnia (by now a regular ritual). Soon I can hear that Mom and Dad have come home from bowling. As usual, I try my best to eavesdrop. Except that, this particular time, I don't have to try hard at all. A huge fight is in progress, audible right from the moment the front door to our apartment bangs shut. As I struggle to make sense of it, what am I learning? My mother has had an affair with a family friend.

My. Mother. Has. Had. An. Affair. Omigod, before I know what my legs are doing, I'm racing out to the living room, looking ridiculous because big tears are running down my face while I'm glaring — positively glaring, like fire's coming out of my eyes — glaring at both parents, while a shaky scared voice yells out of my mouth. What do I tell them? "I heard it all. I understand what you're talking about!"

No more can I say, but they get the point, staring back at me in horror before I proceed to do what my mother has been teaching me to do for years. First, the stomping run back to my bedroom, then the definitively angry door slam. Finally, I leap onto my bed, stomach downward, where my body practically shakes the mattress, I'm sobbing that hard.

"I'm in the trauma zone now." That's my inner refrain.

Also jostling through my mind are bits of *Anna Karenina* and *Madame Bovary*, the two main books we had to read this semester in English class; and for the first time it occurs to me how maybe people who have affairs aren't only exotic fictional women in France and Russia, which might be why Mrs. Lacrouts chose these books for us kids to study before we graduate high school.

Soon, my bedroom door opens. Dad turns on the light, and he comes in to comfort me. (Or, just maybe, himself.) Sulkily I prop myself up on one elbow, looking at him; while my father, naked as usual once evening starts, is sitting atop my bed covers, his back propped up against the wall, with tears glistening in his green eyes. Dad spends maybe 20 minutes with me, asking if I'm alright and then pouring out all his feelings.

Okay, this is what parents do. I know this. Yet somehow his talking like this seems weird to me, weirder even than the Sunday morning when I passed by him on the way to the kitchen, while he was taking a nap on the living room couch. All of a sudden, up comes this thing with his body that, later, I learn the name for: an *erection*.

Somehow this conversation about my mother, having sex! With another man! This topic seems even more shocking to me than watching my Dad sleep naked. Although obviously I'm getting the nakedness treat this time, too. Especially repulsive to me, on this occasion, is Dad's apparent belief that he is now helping *me*.

In the days that follow, I adjust; my parents do too. They promise me they won't get a divorce. But guaranteed, both of them will remain desperately unhappy for the rest of their lives. Or something. I still love these people, my only parents, after all. However, I sense that an old kind of trust has been broken; meaning, a kind of trust that I didn't used to know I had; breaking it has brought home to me how important trust is, though.

In the aftermath of Trauma Night, I form an ideal that married people ought to be able to develop a kind of trust; specifically, a trust strong enough to prevent them from sneaking around and cheating, and then hurting each other. Seems to me, life has suddenly turned grim. I wonder, will I ever be happy again?

But then months pass and I realize that, sure, I'm still happy. Maybe my attitude toward life is like that of my classmate Donna Benjamin. (Incidentally, what are the odds of having a class of just 16 kids and two of them are named Donna?)

Besides Donna Avery, the writer, I do have this other friend in school, Donna Benjamin. And one day, when we're all at recess in school, she starts to snort and scoff and brag all at once.

Because yesterday her Dad got her a special ticket to the Ed Sullivan Show, where the Beatles performed for the first time.

"It was terrible," she tells me and the rest of the girls. "It was fake. The applause was fake. Lights would go on, telling us to applaud. And some man from the TV show sat with us in the audience, off to the side; he kept telling us to scream, and he was gesturing too, pushing us to scream louder and louder.

"So, yeah, I guess it was a big deal that I got to see the Beatles, now that they're starting to become famous. And I did like hearing them sing, but that show wasn't like it seemed, you know? I'm so disgusted."

Donna and me, both! Life gives you a treat, like a family you trust in. But then, sometimes, it winds up tasting as bad as burned potatoes.

CHAPTER 17

Smoke Damage

Ever since my family moved to Flushing, I've had my own room. But when I moved here I was seven. By now the free ride is over. Ever since starting high school, I have been given a chore. In order to build *maturity* (whatever that is) I've been placed in charge of cleaning up my bedroom. Totally up to me is how well (which means badly) and how often (which means almost never).

Messy goes with being a writer, which I've decided to become, especially because my life changed forever after reading *A Portrait of the Artist as a Young Man* by James Joyce.

Which is why, like any teenager, I've fastened a poster of some cute guy on my bedroom wall. Only, in my case, it's the centerfold from a book on Picasso that a relative gave me. You could say, that great artist is my ceiling pin-up. Yes, Questing Reader, I've chosen two big, shiny pages, from an oversized black-and-white book. Each page features one of Picasso's eyes. Through some photography trick, these eyes have been made so enormous that each one fills an entire page, about 8 ½ by 11 inches.

Amazingly, I've managed to remove this centerfold of my book, and done this without ripping anything, and then somehow I've succeeded at fastening those artist's eyes onto my ceiling -- those huge, staring eyes. It consoles me, staring at back at them in the dim light of my bedroom. When I can't fall asleep,

Picasso's eyes are almost enough to make me look forward to each night's long bout of insomnia.

And thus I'm like any All-American teenager who insists on arranging her bedroom just so. What if you asked me, "Isn't your choice of decor a bit strange?"

I would answer indignantly, "No, and there's no point in explaining any of this to you, because if I had to tell you in words? That means you couldn't ever understand."

Actually, nobody asks such impertinent questions. Perhaps that's because nobody but family usually visits my personal room. If I did have any friends worth inviting to visit, they could instantly tell that I'm a writer-in-progress. My highly independent bedroom has become an artistic refuge, especially my pile of things on the gray carpet, a pile in the center of my bedroom that's ignored as much as the proverbial elephant in the room... unless I happen to be looking for something.

Plenty can be found within that personal pile of mine, since this is where I put clothes after undressing. On a typical day my small mountain of independence is ripe with sweaty blouses and rumpled skirts, all the clothes I'm forced to wear for school. *Old socks and panties galore on the floor.* This sounds so good it could almost be an advertising jingle on TV, couldn't it?

What do I daintily avoid adding to this heap? My favorite everyday slacks and blouses, which I prefer to hang up. Since these are, after all, my real clothes, unlike the silly skirts and dresses that you've got to wear to high school. Eventually laundry on the floor will be washed by me, with much grumbling. But first it receives a comfortable lodging along with tasty treats: snack leftovers on plates plus leftover junk food a la carte, as nature intended, meaning "Just about everywhere," especially lots of Peppermint Pattie wrappers.

What else is piled in? School assignments that I'll eventually pack up for school. *You name it, go claim it.* Questing Reader, you could consider that is my slogan for the sport of foraging to retrieve homework. At least, I can usually manage to pull out whatever it was that I looked for. Regardless of outcomes, I take pride in the great artistic flair and adventurousness being symbolized by my bedroom's big and glorious *Gush Pile.*

Grown to my full height by now, I stand next to my Gush Pile and enjoy how it stands nearly as tall as me, which means five feet, two inches. Mostly I'm fond of my creation, except when I can't find a school assignment due that morning, which causes me to do a desperate last-minute search, typically a jerky flinging and flopping of various objects until I emerge triumphant with my limp essay. Or whatever.

However, it's serene in my bedroom, one Saturday morning at 10 a.m., as I sprawl on my bed, reading a novel. In the background, I hear a knock on the front door, a serious-sounding knock. Then another. Since nobody else answers the door, I run over and open it. There's my friend Annette, looking strange, talking fast and not in normal sentences.

"Fire" is one word I pick out.

And then "Fire" again.

"Everybody has to get out!" she says, when it suddenly registers in my mind that technically I am not in Jane Austen's world right now, and there's a strong possibility that everybody in my apartment must exit NOW.

Dad is at work. Mom and Amy come outside with me, looking terrified and oblivious, respectively. But all of us clearly are safe. Soon as I can, I drop them and go watch the unfolding spectacle with my best friends from the neighborhood, Annette and Maureen, and the rest of the gang. Over the next couple of hours, the drama builds, although it's always clear that the building itself will not burn to the ground. It's solid brick.

Three screaming red firetrucks arrive. Unexpectedly, so do masses of people, until a gossipy crowd forms, maybe 200 strong, standing near the firetrucks on 78th Avenue. A fire in your apartment building? Surely this is what my Mom's psychiatrist would call *a trauma*. And yet, to me, a worse trauma is hearing and watching all these people from the neighborhood, mostly total strangers, gathered as if cheering at a sporting event.

Will they see anyone leap, naked, from a burning window? Maybe even be licked to death by flames, right in front of their eyes? Evidently this prospect is more entertaining than watching TV shows, which are only black-and-white. Normally so unfriendly, these strangers: usually when I encounter them on the neighborhood sidewalks, they won't smile back, not even when I pass next to them and toss them my shiniest grin. Believe me, I've tried, which has often caused me to wonder, "How can human beings turn out to be so uninterested in other human beings?" And, also, "Will I ever meet people who are friendly?"

Now we've got interested people all right. They're extremely interested, and in what? A smell like a girl scout marshmallow roast gone horribly, horribly wrong. For sure, the sight of these gossipy strangers scares me more than the fire itself. Although I'll admit, the score is nearly a tie.

Eventually my friends and I figure out that we'll get the best view by running around to the back window side of the apartment building. It's located near communal clotheslines, directly in back of my building. That big backyard rectangle, the size of a tennis court, contains white clotheslines; clotheslines propped up by poles, row upon row of clotheslines. I've always had a warm feeling toward this friendly place, where mothers chit-chat while hanging up their wet laundry with wooden clothespins.

More than that, the clothesline place has inspired me with a wonder-filled memory. You see, Questing Reader, that happened one winter snowstorm many years ago. When I went outside to play, I found mountains of snow, a bright snow that formed perfect drifts for climbing, a unique snow landscape that inspired me to hang and swing from the heavy clotheslines, playing like a monkey in a bright-white jungle.

No carefree joy now though, let alone a sense of miracles in the making. Now, standing with my friends, I stare up at my third-floor window and see the smoke rising. This smoke is even uglier than the crud from cigarettes, that icky Pall Mall tobacco smoke that is apparently required for full maturity, that repulsive smoke which the grownups in my life are constantly blowing right in my face.

Watching smoke from the fire, it's a wicked and different kind of burning. Seems to me that now I know tragedy or, at least, worry. It's the kind of worry I've heard for years in the voices of grownups, their worry being something I've never sought to understand before, yet now maybe I can understand something about that harsh kind of worry.

All this stinking, grimy smoke is burning up what exactly? Could it ruin:

- ➤ Dad's complete collection of wonderful records, his very favorite thing in all of life?
- ➤ What about my favorite sweater, a soft tan, made of fake fur and cute-cute-cute?
- ➤ And how much will be ruined? Where will my family sleep tonight?

Even my dreaded insomnia ritual seems dear to me now, comforting like an old teddy bear whose smelly stuffing comes out sometimes... but you can always stuff it back in and, besides, it's still my bear.

Looking around at us spectators on the ground, I notice Annette, next to me. She's worrying, too. Funny, usually my friend Annette looks so mature, and confident, with her figure that's already 39-29-39 and drives the boys crazy, including my Jimmy Lovelace. Now Annette simply looks sixteen and scared. Like me, I guess.

With a sudden heave-ho, glass shatters. Next, a burning mattress is thrown out the second-story window, tossed out from the bedroom directly beneath my own. I'll never forget the sour, bitter smell of ugliness in that mattress, almost as if it brands my soul.

The mattress comes from the Sophy's apartment where Hugette, the mother, is so close to the ancient grandmother who never speaks English. Plus, there's noisy little Douglas, the toddler they think is so cute; also Christine, slightly my friend, whose cries are the loudest sounds you'll ever hear in the whole apartment building, screams that fade to whimpers when her father beats her, crying sometimes in French and other times in English and always with a kind of sound that I never want to believe can exist.

Little Emmett is the family's middle child. He lives in that downstairs apartment, too. Within a day I learn from Annette that he's the one who caused the fire. Turns out, the kid likes to play with matches and on Saturday he lit up his bed, showing off for Douglas. Then that nasty Emmett, with his sullen little face, went out to play... leaving all the rest of us to deal with that big scare.

How long does it take for the horrible smell of burning to fade away? Weeks in reality. But in my memory, never. And yet, for me, one unexpected sweetness comes from it all. Unlike the Sophy's apartment, which has burned straight through to the charred-wood foundation, my family's apartment survives the fire just fine, except for a bit of smoke damage.

Ironically the Sophy family lacks fire insurance, although the dad is (according to my own Dad) a sleazy insurance salesman who's never bothered to cover his own family by buying insurance. While my so-responsible father *did* purchase fire insurance for us, and thus it happens that, exactly one Saturday after the big fire, he asks me to go survey my bedroom for smoke damage.

Blithely I report back to him, "Nope. I didn't find any."

Ernie says, "Not so fast. Did you look in the closet?"

Shrugging with my well-honed teenage annoyance, I go back to inspect my bedroom closet. What an unusual experience it is for me to enter my closet at all, since mostly my wardrobe exists in the Gush Pile. But in I go. Clothes hangers in front are my everyday slacks, which I must remove to get down to the walls.

Onto my bed goes this first layer. Then my older closet layers emerge: first, fancy dresses, almost never worn; next, outgrown school dresses -- I removed them, flinging them flung onto my bed. By now I begin to feel fascinated, as if becoming some kind of closet archeologist.

In the increasingly musty-smelling depths of my closet, I find loads of outgrown shoes, and then the deeply dusty treasures: Long-forgotten games in cardboard boxes, like Monopoly and Clue, Sorry and Parcheesi; the roller skates I used to clip onto my shoes and then use to race my way around the block, playing percussion on the noisy pavement, clatter-bang-whirr-clunk. Skating so loudly, how fearless I'd feel, and how free!

Also, my old pogo stick has fallen into the back of my closet, against one corner. Pulling out that wonderful pogo stick, I remember the day when I used it to bounce all the way around the block, feeling the remarkable strength of my leg muscles thanks to all that stair-climbing at U.N.I.S. This reminds me of the funniest thing, how in one glorious afternoon of jumping I completely ruined my brand-new pair of shoes. Coming back home, I hear my mother sigh, "These are very expensive shoes. And look at them now."

My mother almost never scolds me, but I fully expect that now will be one of those times. Instead, she shocks me by playfully dangling the shoes downward by holding the laces. That way you can see how the soles have been completely worn down from contact with that wonderful pogo stick. Then my Mom, so athletic back when a girl herself, looks at me with a new respect. Proudly she says, "I'll buy you some new shoes tomorrow."

Just like that, for a moment, those athletically destroyed, old-new shoes of mine look as glorious as a sports trophy — at least, the closest thing to a sports trophy that this not-so-great athlete will ever receive in her life.

Once my closet is fully empty, I discharge my responsibility, sweeping my eyes from left to right (and back), then down to up (and back). Not a bit of smoke damage! Until suddenly I realize with a pang very much like hunger, "It's gone."

What is it that I am *not* seeing?

Something I'm hardly able to remember, let alone manage to see now… And yet a faraway memory tickles my mind, like an old song I'm starting to hum. Deep into my closet, I crawl. Then I sit down.

That's when I remember a place where I used to go. Often. All the way back when I was little, in second grade, that long ago. With a rush of memory, I recall how I used to crawl into my closet, passing through that bit of wall right there at the back… and then I'd enter a hidden place that was sacred. Whenever I needed to, I could go back to that better place, just by using a kind of travel portal built into the wall in back of my closet.

Yes, I had a certain kind of power back then: I could come and go as I wished. No longer can I remember what used to happen there, not a thing. Usually, my memory is excellent. Especially for anything that pulls me away from everyday life! Only this time I draw a blank, except for a strong feeling that mixes sweetness and loss.

If I can't go back to that place, at least I'm so very glad that once upon a time I saw It. Stood in It. Flew in it. Felt It. And breathed It.

"Thank you, Emmett Sophy," I think. "If it weren't for you, that memory would have disappeared even more completely, until I would never be able to find it again. It may be the most beautiful thing I know, even if I don't quite know why."

CHAPTER 18

Becoming A Writer, Damply

Have you ever wondered what is the most wonderful way to fall asleep? Let me tell you, Questing Reader.

Just lie in bed the way that I do these days, sweetly sixteen; not expecting to fall asleep any time soon but resigned to lying comfortably in bed, listening to music. With my bedroom door open, just enough light streams in for me to look toward the ceiling whenever I wish, and then I'm greeted by the eyes of Picasso, that great artist.

What has he painted? Actually, I haven't a clue, because in my family we're not big museum goers. Sure, I still have that book from which the eye photographs were pulled out. But the truth is, I've never once read a word of that book. All I needed was what I found right away, those two centerfold pictures I needed so much, rare glimpses into a great artist's eyes.

Lying in bed every night, I'll look up at Picasso. He's always sympathetic company, and available whenever I want him. Eventually I'll let my eyes close, drifting toward sleep while lingering over whatever mystery music my father has chosen to play in the living room. Vocal music is my favorite, with songs of love and longing, endurance and boldness. Usually, I can't understand a word. The singing could be any language, and that's seldom English.

This allows me up to listen even more freely, and so does my near-sleep state. Listening each night, it's as though x-rays open up within my ears, revealing deep feelings within each singer's heart until, almost physically, I feel the swelling or fall of each note. Questing Reader, have you ever noticed how certain singers can cram a performance fuller even than an over-packed suitcase? I mean, the kind of suitcase you must sit on, and squash down, before it can close. Thanks to kids I've met at U.N.I.S., it seems as if I can feel the home countries of each singer, like the Italian-ness of handsome-voiced Beniamino Gigli, and the musically correct yet irrepressible coloratura soprano Melitza Korjus, from Austria.

Sometimes I drift toward sleep along with *Music of Bulgaria*. These choral folk songs teach me about people from Eastern Europe, how they depend on working together. I love, and learn from, Phillip Koutev's chorus as it chimes the air, like ringing a bell of belonging.

You know, movie stars and other celebrities usually strike me as fake, arousing no interest whatsoever. By contrast, these singers who guide me toward sleep — they have come to feel like real friends to me, even serving as teachers of truth. Because it's as though each of these voices tells me about that person's way of being.

➤ Miriam Makeba opens me up to the bright soul of South Africa.

➤ Eleanor Steber sings Mahler's Kindertoten lieder in a way which teaches that I, too, will be able to survive tragedy, should I ever need to find new strength.

➤ Best of all, an ecstatic British soprano in Bournemouth brings contagious joy to *Rejoice Greatly*, showing me how to feel the very sweetest connection to Handel's *Messiah*.

***

Apart from all my one-way friendships with the world's great singers, let's get real. How's my social life doing?

Not too great. So far, I've had only one date, stiff and forgettable -- except for beforehand, while *making plans* over the phone. Questing Reader, I promise you, that got my dating life off to an great start. What happened was this. A boy in the neighborhood, Cliff, had asked for my phone number and I'd given it to him. Obviously, The Call was coming!

Excited at first, soon I felt overwhelmed at the prospect of making an actual date. So I hatched a plan, begging my sister for help. Long story short, when Cliff finally called, my job was to listen over our home's phone extension, holding my breath in suspense, while Amy pretended to be me. Confidently she chatted with Cliff, and they set up the official date before hanging up.

Lucky for me, my sister's voice sounds exactly like mine, plus we did some serious rehearsing. As for the date itself? About as memorable as water pouring through a very self-conscious sieve.

By contrast, I'm totally uninhibited at... listening. Especially listening to my very favorite aria, so French, from *The Pearlfishers*, where a tenor sings about falling in love at first sight. "Yes, it's her." Incidentally, Questing Reader, please don't feel awkward if you haven't heard about that opera, or any of the other kinds of music I've told you about in this chapter. My father was a music nerd and raised me accordingly.

How about my teenage attempts to make music on my own? Although I don't aim to become a professional musician, I do take violin lessons. Never do I miss a day's practice. Practicing faithfully every day, for the last several months I always play the slow movement of Bach's Double Concerto. Every day I make the same mistakes. For the life of me, I don't understand why that happens.

The art of practicing music is an impossible mystery, or so it seems to me. Nobody has ever explained to me how I can get past the hard parts, and my parents have taught me well: never ask for advice about anything. Left to my own devices, here's what I wind up doing:

1. Play vigorously until I get stuck at some tricky notes on the music score.
2. Annoyed, I clap out the correct rhythm. (Although afterward I forget it immediately.)
3. Compromise by playing the notes again. But this time I don't bother to play any set rhythm at all. (Satisfying except for how guilty it makes me feel.)

After using this procedure, I'll tell myself, "Problem solved." Therefore, I'll proceed to start all over, right from the beginning. Surprise! Soon I wind up stuck in the very same place. Honestly, if I didn't like my violin so much, I'd give up playing altogether.

Only I really do love playing that violin, slowly drawing my bow across the strings, feeling vast flows of emotion whenever I play. Also, Mom encourages me. She says "People have told me it's hard to listen to somebody practicing the violin, because usually they squeak. But you always sound beautiful to me."

Clearly my mother approves. While the original composer isn't in the room with me to complain, since he's J.S. Bach, who happens to be dead! So why shouldn't I feel free to take as long as I like with each note, feeling whatever I need to feel, then considering that I've put in a good day's practice?

How I wish I could have that kind of freedom while playing in my little orchestra at music school. Questing Reader, are you surprised that a *musician* like me has managed to get into an orchestra? Here's how it happens. On my violin teacher's recommendation, I start taking Saturday classes, along with my sister, at the Dalcroze School in Manhattan. Since my parents spare no expense when helping Amy and me, the two of us begin leaping around in Eurhythmics Class. Supposedly, this is helping me to develop a great sense of rhythm.

Except that, just as certain people are *tone deaf,* I might possibly be *time deaf.* However, a bonus with Eurhythmics is automatic admission to the Saturday afternoon orchestra, where they let me play as one of the second fiddles. All semester long at Dalcroze, we prepare for a concert, practicing our one piece of music over and over. Finally, one Saturday the parents come to hear us perform; although mine don't, which is fine by me. Performing is intense enough without being noticed by anyone.

Encouragingly, I notice how lovely the first few measures sound, like a real orchestra. There I sit on my folding chair, leaning over my instrument, with the Telemann score right before my eyes, when a wave of feeling moves through me: the inexpressible beauty of how we're all playing together, and how I've got a real music stand in front of me, with real music to play; and yes, how I'm in an orchestra, a real orchestra; and this time we even have an audience.

Oh, my heart grows so grateful, excessively thrilled, until cool tears of fulfillment begin to roll down my cheeks. Eventually I'm ready to stop weeping and resume playing. Only, to my surprise, the concert is over now. Parents are clapping. Oh, dear! And thus, I sit out my one and only orchestral performance.

Questing Reader, lest it appear that I'm a total nincompoop, the space-out aspect of my life only appears with music, writing, and poetry, and maybe some other times, too. But…. By this time in my life, I've done cheerleading for a local Little League team; consistently slammed my opponents at squash (a local version, played with tennis racquets on a handball court); and I've even served as captain of the sad-'n-small   U.N.I.S. basketball team.

As captain of that basketball team, I have one proud moment. In our only game with another school, I'm zealously working the court as a guard when two much bigger girls — each one maybe as tall as an alarming 5'7" — these menacing girls pull me aside and threaten me.

"You're way too aggressive as a guard. If you don't dial it back, after the game we're going to take you outside and beat you up." Golly, at the time of this writing, that threat remains my proudest sports moment (along with the trophy I've already told you about, those new shoes I managed to wreck with my great pogo stick prowess).

Academically, there are some bright spots too. I've passed five British-style college entrance exams (O Levels) and received a rare award from the Alliance Française for language study.

Also, taking advantage of a special U.N.I.S. elective, I've studied Russian after school, becoming the only kid in that class to not drop out. As a result, my pronunciation is excellent when saying the unbelievably depressing Russian word for *life*. (Questing Reader, catch me live and ask me to tell it to you any time. I look forward to seeing your reaction.)

What else? I win a tiny brag as a National Merit Scholar Semi-Finalist.

***

You get the idea, Questing Reader. I'm not altogether a loser, just a bit of a dreamer. And what else about me at age 16 is still pretty much about dreaming? Love.

Which brings me to confess a gigantic crush on my classmate, Mark Seligson. Why do I love him so? Partly because of his thick, straight chestnut hair and matching gorgeous eyes with those huge dark lashes that some boys get — which is so unfair, isn't it?

Mostly I've fallen in love with Mark through his essays. Because every week my English teacher forever, Mrs. Lacrouts, assigns us to write a new essay. Later she reads parts of the best ones out loud in front of the whole class, which is how I come to totally fall in love with Mark. By now I'm pretty sure of what I want to be when I grow up, a poet. And Mark loves poetry, too. Once he even gets into trouble on account of poetry.

Questing Reader, here's the story of his brave, brave act of rebellion. Mark fastened a sign to one of our tall window poles. Then he stuck that sign out the window, like a flag, so just about every student in the school could see it. On that sign Mark has written, "The active mind needs poetry. Join the Walt Whitman Society."

Through this very un-U.N.I.S.-like act of rebellion, Mark gets into big trouble. Also he has to take down the sign. This daring act only makes Mark, more than ever, My Poetry Hero. Resulting in such shyness around him, never once do I tell him how much I admire his essays and, especially, his sign. Such vision, trying to add poetry to our plodding old school!

Dramatically, even the possibility of ever telling him this... dies. Because one day, over lunch break, one of the girls tells me that Mark is being expelled. Can't be helped, since he has been caught in the boy's bathroom doing the unforgiveable. Smoking a cigarette!

Look, this is 1964. Kids at U.N.I.S. can't do awful things like that. Of course, he must be expelled. Anguished, I leave my lunch on the cafeteria table and race up to our home room. Boldly I run over to Mark's desk and find... Be still my trembling heart! Somehow, I manage to locate his big blue loose-leaf binder, containing essays penned by My Poetry Hero.

Does it ever occur to me to use this looseleaf as a place to write down my telephone number? Or maybe I could do something even more outlandish and scribble down an invitation like this: "Mark, I'm old enough to date now, and I'm pretty sure my parents would let me. So why don't you call me up and maybe we could go out together?"

No, that is way too aggressive for a girl like me. At least I manage to grab myself a consolation prize. Turning over the pages in Mark's loose-leaf binder, I find one of his brilliant essays, rip it right out, hide it in my green bookbag. Shamelessly take it home with me. Yes, I steal.

It is a beautiful essay to have and to hold and to cherish and, especially, to read over and over again. The haunting beauty of Mark's book report about *Eyeless in Gaza* by Aldous Huxley! Oh, the wit of that boy's writing, and his searching soul! Obviously I will love him forever. Yet nothing can be done, at least nothing that occurs to me. Mark leaves my life like another batch of white pull candy that I'll never be able to taste. He leaves in disgrace, far as I know -- saying goodbye to nobody.

Somehow my life does go on. Quite normally, actually. Except for what sort-of happens one Friday night on my way to a Girl Scout meeting. Travel this incident along with me, Questing Reader. To set the scene, the reason I'm talking a walk at night is that I'm going to join my Intermediate Troop's Friday meeting, walking to Parkway Village, not far from my old school building.

Growing up fast now, I'm allowed to walk on my own, in the dark, to the troop leader's house. Three miles each way isn't too far, given my strong U.N.I.S. legs. Pondering this and that, gradually I notice a gentle rain falling. Then just as gently, I begin to notice a special feeling within me, as though everything is alive. I mean, really alive, from inside.

Questing Reader, you couldn't imagine a bigger contrast from the way I usually feel, which is terminally separated from everyone else; physically kind of clunky and chubby; emotionally wearing my everyday outfit of teenage sorrow, decorated with a few special touches of insecurity — like how my Mom might wear a necklace to show off her black dress.

Yet now, in this gentle fall rain, all my everyday feelings simply wash away, leaving me with a quiet way of being that is entirely new, a kind of singing joy. Yes, a silent kind of singing joy, and it's everywhere. Maybe it's like what they mean by the name of that famous Christmas carol, *Silent Night*.

Silent, where you can't hear anything on the outside, but inside you are singing with every fiber of your being. And you're connected, through joy, to every stranger near you, even if nobody stops to speak. Not that I wish to talk, either. Instead, I stand still, mid-block, on Queens Boulevard, while listening for something that can't quite be heard physically. Yet somehow the sweetest silence is peeking out through the whoosh and rushing of other pedestrians, and despite how loudly the cars are squeaking, due to the wet roads.

At least I know what to do, since I'm carrying pencil and paper for making notes at my Girl Scout meeting. Moving until I stand beneath a traffic light, for maximum visibility while writing, I pull out a piece of that paper and hold it against my handbag for support. Then I write a description of what's happening now, which is just like a poem: how I'm standing in that singing rain mixed with silence, and everything looks so beautiful; with the lights on the cars all turned into rubies and emeralds, and everything sparkling with the singing joy.

Such a silly girl I am! Ridiculous looking, too, with my clothing soaked through and raindrops dripping off the end of my nose. And yet dignity matters even less to me now... than usual. Which is helpful, particularly since my mouth starts stretching wide into a gigantic grin. If my very visible teeth could tumble out from sheer happiness, I'd let them. After writing all the words I can find, I fold up my soggy wad of paper and tuck it into my pocket – a new writing treasure that can become precious to me, like Mark Seligson's essay.

CHAPTER 19

Finding WHAT in the Hem of My Skirt?

History is still one damned thing after another, at least according to Mr. Sullivan, who's still my history teacher, which means that history class all my senior year will repeat his favorite examples of "one damned thing after another." Such as "The Holy Roman Empire wasn't holy or Roman or even an empire."

Every year, the feudal system is where we begin to study European history. The feudal system includes an annual oath of fealty that a vassal swears to his lord. Following that lesson, our class goes rollicking through the industrial revolution into the emergence of modern nations, and then on to World War I. That's Mr. Sullivan's annual sequence of lessons, each one punctuated by the usual jokes. Yes, he tells us exactly the same jokes we've already heard from him, three years straight.

At least I manage to spring one little joke on my world-weary history expert. One of my college entrance exams, an achievement test, is in history. Apparently, I score the highest grade in my class. This would be due to many conversations I've had with my father, who's fascinated by history and has talked about it with me for years.

Probably my modest success perplexes Mr. Sullivan, since he pegged me as a dullard four years ago and hasn't changed his mind since. No doubt he thinks the College Board just inflicts "one more damned thing after another"... on *him*.

Finishing high school at U.N.I.S., what do I love? The language classes. In French we learn about life by reading *Les Fleurs du Mal (The Flowers of Evil)* by Charles Baudelaire, because it's so helpful for us teenagers to read the musings of an angry, drug-crazed poet from 100 years ago. In Spanish we're treated to *La Rebellión de las Masas (The Revolt of the Masses)*, providing encouragement in case we're planning to become revolutionaries.

And then I've got Mr. Quigley, my teacher for both Math and Physics, speaking Greek to me -- but with an adorable Irish lilt. Unfortunately, Mr. Quigley never seems to use his musical voice to connect to his students, not even in my physics class which, being an unpopular science elective, includes only four of us kids.

Questing Reader, here's my favorite moment with this teacher. Picture physics class in May of my senior year and well, well, well... what happens? For the first, and only time, ever, Mr. Quigley appears to be a tiny bit interested in me. While demonstrating a physics experiment, quite suddenly, he realizes exactly what he needs right now: a pin, a straight pin, the kind of pin used for sewing.

And so Mr. Quigley looks me straight in the eye and asks politely, "Could you please lend me a pin?"

When I looked confused, he explains. "Back home, all the girls your age carry sewing supplies. They're tucked inside the hems of your skirts: a needle, a bit of thread, and some pins. So you can readily find these things for me."

When I stare at him blankly, he explains the obvious:

"Because you never know when a person might need you to help out with some mending."

I blush, all the way down to the hem of my green corduroy skirt. My teacher is thinking about the inside of my hem? More complication: Obviously this man is gay; even my Grandma Irene might be able to tell, when it comes to Quigley. Altogether, there is something deeply troubling about Irish girls my age being doomed to serve as perpetual handmaidens, proffering their sewing supplies.

Grownups! My favorite times in school are really *after* school, unsupervised by grownups. Such as when I walk over to the Museum of Modern Art, with its free admission.

Whenever I want upliftment as a writer, I'll go there after school. Specifically, I'll make a beeline for the Water Lilies Room. I find "my bench," where you can sit and let yourself tumble into Monet's paintings. His amazing depictions of water lilies adorn all four walls of this room, and usually I'm the only person there. Granted, this Flushing girl has never been anywhere close to a real water lily. These French ones are gigantic, as if they come from another planet, and a very dreamy world indeed, a world that I would prefer to inhabit. But no repining; at least I can visit those lilies whenever I wish.

Being nearly grown-up by now brings me wonderful freedom, but I'm also more aware of problems in society. Between you and me, Questing Reader, I'm even slightly tempted to believe that Mr. Sullivan might be right about history being a series of meaningless events. Scary events, for sure! Of course, everyone in America today is terrified of Communists and The Bomb. Even though we laugh at songs by Tom Lehrer or watch *That Was the Week That Was* on TV, it seems like everybody expects World War III to start any day.

Lying awake at night, I'll hear airplanes fly overhead. Dad has explained to me that our apartment lies along the flight path for both of New York's two big airports, La Guardia and Idlewild, which we used to visit for fun when I was little; now that I'm grown up, it's just an airport, and it has been renamed *Kennedy Airport.*

Given my father's explanation, hearing so many planes shouldn't bother me. Yet what happens when I hear the sound of planes while lying in bed? It gives me the strangest feeling, like I'm back in Europe or someplace, and it's World War II, and the planes carry bombs.

Of course, that's ridiculous. Nothing violent happens to me, not ever; if anything, my life could be considered horribly boring; and ever since my tonsils came out, I've been perfectly healthy, too, as strong as a horse. Unfortunately, my Daddy is not. Last year he had a heart attack, and recently a doctor has given him something new called a "Pacemaker."

After coming home from the hospital with his Pacemaker, Ernie has been on a diet. Every night he drinks loads of diet soda, as if that could work like a magic potion for slenderness. *No-Cal* soda has newly arrived at our supermarket, available in flavors like (Imitation) Orange, colored a violent shade of wax fruit. To me it tastes like liquid plastic. Even weirder is *Metrecal*, also a new fad, packaged as a miraculous kind of diet cookie, quite revolting unless you prefer a taste like "virtuous medicine."

Mom tries a Metrecal diet, so do too. Once. Metrecal doesn't work for either of us, except for one thing. Every bite of those square, hard "cookies" deposits within me… several new ounces of fatness guilt. On the positive side, so much is delightful in my almost-completely-grown-up life now. For instance, I'm so relieved that lately my Aunt Carol has been doing well. She has a job. She still lives in her sophisticated apartment near Lincoln Center. And now she has a regular boyfriend, too, Paul.

Mom worries because they both drink so much, but I think Paul is cool. He has told me about the time when, once, he got to be friends with the poet Dylan Thomas. Here's how that happened: Together they were locked up in jail after a party that got too loud. Jail was great, Paul said, because he tayed up all night listening to Dylan telling him stories. Then, first thing next morning, they were released, no big deal.

When Paul and Carol come over for dinner, he likes to joke that my name is "Lolita." Apparently, this has something to do with a popular novel by Vladimir Nabokov. Mom doesn't like Paul's jokes, but I don't mind. Mostly I'm glad that my brave Aunt Carol has found someone to love her.

Now that I'm in my late teens I can really appreciate how great she is. Questing Reader, out of all the stories she tells us about her many jobs, this one is my favorite: A collection agency has hired her to call up people in debt for lots of money. Carol is supposed to scare them into paying, but the company doesn't supervise much, so she decides to do something different.

First, she calls each debtor, announcing, "I'm calling about your unpaid bill." Invariably the debtor starts complaining how tough life is, giving one excuse after another for why the debt isn't paid yet.

Then Aunt Carol shocks the debtor by announcing, "I understand completely. Don't feel any pressure to pay back that money. Far as we're concerned, you have all the time in the world."

To teenage me, that's hilarious. *Mad Magazine* is also hilarious. Every chance I get, I do what I can to laugh, and my sister Amy laughs along with me. At this point she really is my best friend, and we stick together during the hard times. Like when Grandma Gisela gets sick! During our final visit, she looks tiny in her hospital bed, more like a doll than a person, and I get a horrible feeling that soon she is going to die.

Which she does.

Afterward Grandpa Hugo moves into a nursing home. By now his health isn't so hot, either. Besides, he doesn't know how to cook for himself. The last time I see Hugo is after he moves into that nursing home and I think, "In this place he won't last long."

True, it turns out. True but very sad. Around the very same time, my other Grandpa dies too. Goodbye, Grandpa Sussman. I've only met him twice. He wasn't a very good father to Sue, far as I can tell. Still, the news makes my mother cry a lot.

As if all that dying weren't enough, death gets Nana, too. One day I come home from school only to be greeted by the news that she suddenly dropped dead. Mom explains that Nana Irene went to the hospital for a simple checkup. While there, she caught something and died from it. Basically, she died from going to the hospital for a checkup. Life can be so unsettling, when you can't predict what will happen, not in a million years.

The night I learn of her death, I receive a different kind of surprise. One minute, I'm lying in bed, staring up at Picasso's eyes and settling in for my predictable hours of insomnia. Then, what happens next? In a sudden way (yet not a startling way, somehow) I see Nana again, right there in my bedroom. She doesn't look like a ghost or anything weird, more like herself framed by a Christmas tree ornament.

Questing Reader, did you ever see the kind of ornament with a colorful oval center and, around it, a gold-ish metal that terminates in tall spires on top and bottom?

Nana's face is glowing right there in the middle, like she's in the center of that kind of Christmas ornament with the two spires. Only her ornament is a bright kind of light, all radiant gold, shining around my Nana with a beautiful energy. In its own way, all this feels as normal as anything else that could happen in my life.

We talk in Telepathy, which I haven't done since being a little kid, but the knack comes back instantly. I'm a little embarrassed to tell you, Questing Reader, I don't say anything polite like, "So sorry to hear that you're dead" or even "How ya doin?"

No, in typical fashion, I get right to the point. "Irene, how could you?" I ask.

Then my little packet of thoughts elaborates a bit, scolding her even more, "What were you thinking? How could you have been such a lousy mother to my Mom and Elly and Carol? How could you abandon them like that?"

Irene looks at me then, with her big eyes, always so beautiful, and now looking bluer than ever. Somehow, she's not looking the least bit offended, either. I guess that's because both of us are speaking the language of Telepathy which, for people like us, can't help but be truthful.

Curvy Irene has given Sue a very similar body, and then Sue has given me one with the same kind of shape, but neither of us has inherited those gorgeous blue eyes. I can feel how she's still beautiful in the forever part of her, and for the first time I understand how Grandpa Sussman could have loved her, and my mother loved her once too, and my two aunts, and with the tiniest startle I realized that I kind of love my Nana too.

In a natural sort of way, with no shame, she explains.

"Before I came into the life as Irene, I had many lifetimes as a nun. Altogether, I've had a lot of lifetimes that focused on serving other people, and so it was arranged for me to have this one lifetime just so I could play and enjoy myself, a kind of vacation."

In short, Irene gives me no apology, just the truth. Plus, she sends me a big energy burst of a hug. Then she vanishes.

Even though I never have an experience like that again, somehow that conversation seems perfectly normal to me, nothing like having *a vision.* And how I wish that people could talk like that all the time! I'm so ready to have totally honest conversations with everyone. What Irene has just said, wow! This clears up a lot for me. Instantly my heart opens up and I stop blaming her for the past.

***

Through all four of these family deaths, Amy comforts me, and we draw closer than ever. Our biggest interest, now, is religion.

We're so curious, and now that we're big enough to roam the world, we go everywhere we can go, seeking God. Not just the church and convent across the street, Queen of Peace. We go to a Jewish synagogue in the neighborhood. Then we visit a gorgeous cathedral in Manhattan, St. John the Divine.

Just about every weekend we go to a new house of worship until we find my favorite, the Quaker Meeting House in Flushing, which happens to be the oldest Friends place in all of New York City. We love those meetings.

Back home I seek God by reading, too. Mysteriously, I have acquired a book of poetry by Basho, a Japanese guy from long ago who writes in ways that remind me of the kids' puzzle books with connect-the-dot pictures. His short poems contain the dots. You must connect them for yourself, across what feels like a very big space.

Close to high school graduation, my friend Donna Avery gives me a present, a book about religions of the world. When I turn to Hinduism, it explains the meaning of *reincarnation.*

Reincarnation? Here I am, 17 years old, and nobody has ever mentioned that word before. Now, suddenly, I remember. Of course!

I remember reincarnation. How funny is that? Discovering that word helps me to understand what Nana told me during that goodbye visit, like about her other "lifetimes."

Other books that I'm reading these days are honest, the way I want life to be. By which I definitely don't mean *The Catcher in The Rye*, or any of the Salinger books that are supposed to be telling things from a teen point of view.

Sure, I've read all his bestsellers, and they're kind of addictive, like eating one salty pretzel after another. Only they don't strike me as authentic stories about teenagers, so much as sharing Salinger's self-indulgent fantasy about adolescence, which he couldn't be farther from really remembering.

I want to read about what really matters, which is finding the truth in life. When will I meet somebody who can tell me that? *On the Road* by Jack Kerouac seems to come close, and he thrills me as if I were a fellow pilgrim. I love his stories of beatniks and how they would smoke pot to understand people better. I would love to try that kind of life.

Even better, my favorite books now, when getting ready to graduate high school, are all by Aldous Huxley. Especially *The Doors of Perception,* where he describes taking peyote, which brings him a vision of God. I want that more than anything. Maybe when I get to college?

Meanwhile here's a checklist of life skills that have prepared me for life in college and beyond. For perspective, I'll compare my readiness for life with my classmate Donna, probably the most normal kid I know.

Readiness for Adult Life in America, 1965

Has a Big Brother to Help Her Grow Up
Donna: Yes, two. Plus, a big sister and also a baby sister.

Me: As if!

Can Curl Her Hair, Wears a Hairstyle
Donna: Yes

Me: Huh?

Able to Give Herself a Manicure
Donna: Easy!

Me: Not sure what that is.

Basic Knowledge of Geography, Such as Where She Lives
Donna: Sure.

Me: Nope, unless you count the nearest subway station.

Has Learned How to Drive a Car
Donna: Yes.

Me: Not really.

Shops at a New Kind of Store, a "Mall"
Donna: Probably.

Me: Clueless.

Kisses Well. Has Had Experience
Donna: Definitely.

Me: Do pillows count?

Dress She Wears to High School Graduation
Donna: Thanks to sewing lessons from her Mom, Donna has
    made her own dress. It's a soft white and fits perfectly.

Me: After I saw a pretty white nightgown in Mom's dresser, I
    asked permission to borrow it for my big day. It looks just
    like a Greek toga. Feels just right!

And thus, I graduate, complete with college acceptance and even
a partial scholarship. Maybe in college I'll finally fit in.

At an orientation party with other New Yorkers who are
becoming freshmen, I notice that all the other girls have pierced
ears. Suddenly I'm frantic to get my ears pierced too. Mom
understands perfectly and sends me to the family doctor, who
pierces my ears just right. It's the first time I've ever, ever tried
to wear something fashionable. But for eight years now, I've
been stuck in a big box of a school with kids who began bullying
me in fourth grade. Even after the serious bullying stopped,
around eighth grade, my status has been low, low, low.

Granted, I've always gotten along with the neighborhood kids.
To them, I'm not weird. What will happen with the new kids I
meet in college? Will I make friends? How about God? Will I
even manage to find myself?

PART FOUR. Hippie, My First Real Religion

CHAPTER 20

Be Discreet

"Be discreet," proclaims my residence counselor. During our official College Orientation, discretion is an oft-repeated theme, as we freshmen sit cross-legged on the floor of her dorm room. She's explaining how to succeed at college, and not just for this year but for all four years to come at Brandeis University.

Brandeis (the name sounds like *BRAND-dice*) is my new school, named for the first Jewish Supreme Court Justice. Louis Brandeis gave the school its motto, which I adore, "Truth, even unto its innermost parts."

Such an Orientation! Apparently, I'm in a very liberal college now. Unlike my darling Mark Seligson, I'm allowed to smoke all the cigarettes I want. This good, since I now smoke nearly a pack a day. And am I hearing this right? My residence counselor says that I can smoke pot, too, so long as I don't get caught; plus, I can let boys hang out in my dorm room, and with the door closed!

Even more unimaginable, I could even *live* with a boy in my dorm room; anything goes, so long as I do good schoolwork and *never, ever get caught* — which, I'm now learning, is the literal meaning of "Be discreet." Never before have I known such freedom, built into this incredibly new way of life in a college dorm, where I'm surrounded by hundreds of kids close to my age, and every single one of them juicy-minded, oozing the very Brandeis blend of questing and brains and chutzpah.

Besides, since it's 1965 we can call ourselves "hippies" and act accordingly. Girls and boys alike, many of us, wear our hair long, usually with a part straight down the middle, denoting honesty, obviously. And some of us even choose to go barefoot, which strikes me as such a liberating idea that I pretty much take off my shoes for four years and don't put them on again unless there is snow on the ground. Soon my feet develop such thick calluses, I'm like a hobbit in Tolkien's *Lord of the Ring* books, which happen to be popular right now.

Speaking of liberating, it's hard to describe how great it feels to no longer be living at home. Admitting this to myself is kind of embarrassing, yet here's the truth: I'm practically glowing from sheer relief, despite really wanting to be a good person (which, I know, I know, is supposed to include being a good daughter). Since my parents drove me to college and helped move my boxes of things into the dorm, it has been two months before I've telephoned them even once.

During that call I learn this unsurprising fact, described at length: how my mother cried all the way home, the entire drive from Waltham, Massachusetts to Flushing, New York, maybe four hours straight. So thoroughly unsurprising, to put it mildly! Dad still deals with the Mama-drama every day, but not me, no way, not me anymore. Honestly, is that asking too much? Because I'm a college student now, and I'm allowed to have my own life. So far, Philosophy is my favorite freshman class, so I declare Philosophy as my major.

If anything is going to help me find God, that's philosophy, right?

***

Except what happens, late in that first semester, when I bravely arrange to meet with my advisor from the Philosophy Department? The prospect of talking one-on-one with a professor practically curdles my soul with shyness, curdles it right up like cottage cheese. But which other person could I possibly ask?

So here I find myself, in a room with Professor Santos. Gamely I try on my college student voice, aiming to sound academic yet casual, unlike the too-eager kid whose question isn't the least bit casual.

"Would you, um, perhaps... recommend a book... that could help me to find God?"

Dr. Santos looks sympathetic and so wise, as if requests like mine come to him daily. After briefly rummaging through a shelf filled with big academic tomes, he returns with one selection, hands it to me, and says that I may borrow it. I thank him, then practically run all the way back to my dorm room, clutching that book like a treasure map.

Only what happens after I open that book? Turns out, it's by a cultural anthropologist who describes how differently people in various cultures have manufactured loads of silly ideas about a God.

Apparently, academic rigor can help to elucidate why different groups of people seize upon their foolish ideas. In order to gain true wisdom about God, all that's required is for me to frame each group's search for a higher power by adding a cultural perspective.

Well, maybe Dr. Santos wants to do that. I sure don't. Do I ever read his book?

Of course not, since I might destroy it utterly with my righteous indignation, such as laser-like rays of disdain pulsating out of my eyes and zapping every page. "Sorry sir. I didn't mean to torch your expensive book. It's just that, due to my multiple disagreements with the author's methodology, my eyes began itching in an unaccountable way that I couldn't control."

Not only do I politely return the book in pristine condition, but I change majors... the very next day. To Music. (And then, in coming years, to Sociology. And finally, to English.)

What else can I change? Instead of acting like a pathetically naive, predictable freshman seeker of God, I make a serious resolution. In the future I will keep that Divine search to myself. Outwardly, I'll act like somebody who is naturally discreet. Maybe. as a result, I won't feel so much like a fool.

CHAPTER 21

Fitting Right in with the Nonconformists

I love school, always have, always will, because any classroom feels to me like a sacred place. What do I love, exactly, about a schoolroom? How, right from the first moment, everybody knows we're all about learning; not terribly different from sitting down to a tasty banquet, only the knowledge-food is being cooked right there in the classroom, where amazing ingredients can be summoned out of thin air.

One question from a student and my teacher pulls out a strawberry. More Q&As follow, producing a salami omelet -- like the only recipe my father ever taught me how to cook. Or maybe the class cooks up a lusty casserole (such as my Mom's best family dish, cheddar cheese melting all over the top and, beneath, a luscious combination of spinach and beef and sour cream).

Yum! Now that I'm in college, the quality of knowledge-cooking is better than anything I've tasted yet. Best of all is any class with Professor Allen Grossman, where he speaks with such inspiration, erudition, and relevance. He does this first for my class in Humanities, revealing the inner greatness of the warrior Achilles.

In a different course on England's metaphysical poets, Dr. Gossman takes us on a Magical Mystery Tour led by the likes of George Herbert, an Anglican priest and soul-stirring poet.

Every class, *any* class at Brandeis, is pure delight… except for just one problem. My dream is to become a writer, and yet the only part of writing that I seem to have achieved so far is *Writer's Block*.

Why can't I be practical, like one of my roommates, Jennifer Cassetari? Although she could have become an English major like me, she chose otherwise, and why? Because she used her noodle to think about money; namely, the average incomes of college grads with different majors; and since economists earn the most, that's what she picks. An economist she will be.

Well, I'm determined to become a writer anyhow. Writing is my favorite thing, along with being in a classroom. Although writing on demand has always been hard, to put it mildly. Writing assignments was hard even back in high school, producing those weekly essays for Mrs. Lacrouts, a process that felt like a kind of torture, complete with lots of pencil chewing and even more brow furrowing.

When really, really blocked mentally, what was the most extreme thing I would do? True confession, Questing Reader, just between you and me: I would tear off a small piece of paper from my loose-leaf binder, then eat it.

How sad is that? Chewing paper for inspiration, an inspiration that never materialized. Yet I swear to you, somehow that tasteless wad of paper would bring me hope: like a half-remembered promise that I could taste — almost like a vow — a promise that, if only I wouldn't give up, eventually, I would learn how to let the words flow.

Despite this struggle, starting with writer's block in high school, I do keep on writing. By the time of my high school yearbook, I even get to write the editorial. Unfortunately, this isn't nearly as good as a sonnet published there too, a sonnet written by science whiz kid, my friend Roderick Chu.

He doesn't make a big fuss about wanting to be a writer. Yet Roderick probably has more writing talent in one of his pinky fingernails than I do in my entire self. Really, my photo caption in that yearbook says it all. "Give it an understanding but no tongue." That's me?

Yep, and thus do my writerly aspirations contrast with the sad reality of my life by the time I get to college. Here in college, I even get into trouble on account of my writing. This awkward episode begins with a call from my bank in town, the Waltham bank -- whose name I can never remember because it's only a stupid bank. Besides, truth be told, it feels weird to have my first checking account.

Even weirder, though, is a phone call I receive one afternoon. From the bank manager! "There's a problem," he says. Could I come over right away?

Of course I run there immediately, going as fast as my heart-pounding body can carry me. Soon I'm alone with the bank manager in his fancy office, where he withdraws five pieces of paper from an envelope and lays them down dramatically on his desk, one small piece of paper at a time.

Staring at his expensive-looking, super-solid wooden desk, I see absolutely nothing wrong with those papers. They're five of my checks, the only checks I've written in my entire adult life, an adult life that clearly was supposed to begin automatically when I moved to college. They're just five ordinary-looking checks that I had the money to pay for, so what's the big deal?

"You really don't see anything wrong with those checks?" asks the bank manager. "Would you please take another look?"

If this were a set of words that he wanted me to put into sonnet form, I'd leap at the chance. But this? I'm gawking at papers that show how I wrote checks for pretty small amounts of money, my own money, no embezzlement crime here; so honestly, what's his problem?

At this rate, it seems as if his punishing silence might go on forever, until I look up at the banker's stern face, and I guess he can see that I'm both frightened and totally puzzled, because his own expression seems to gentle up a bit. "Your signature," he says, pointing from one signature line on a check... to the next... and then the next and the next and the next.

"I don't get it," I tell him, ultra-embarrassed by now. Since all I can tell is what I knew before entering this stuffy office in the first place, how I wrote each of these checks, and then signed every one, and I also spelled my name correctly every single time, Laura Sue Rosenbaum.

The bank executive looks at me now with a weary expression, maybe also arranging his face in a way he never has had to arrange it before, not in all his polite years of wearing a suit and tie and the cologne of extreme formality. "Your signature is written differently every single time," he says patiently.

Look, that's hardly news to me. You could say it's the main thing I learned from penmanship class back in fourth grade, and I've been doing the same ever since, writing from different angles and with letters all different sizes, kind of like individual snowflakes drifting beautifully onto on a page.

Patiently, ever so patiently, he tells me, "From now on, you write your name the exact same way every time. That's what a signature is supposed to be. Do you understand?"

After I nod, he tells me, "You can go now."

Walking back to campus, I scuff my shoes on the pavement, feeling beyond dejected. Any kind of writing and me — seems like I'm doomed to fail every time.

Writing failure seems to happen routinely when I've got a college paper to complete. Class after class, and paper after paper, I fuss and worry and persevere. And I keep at my writing despite feeling so stuck I could vomit, except how can you vomit when you have no body?

You see, Questing Reader, having no body is how I feel whenever sitting at my desk, pen in hand. It's as though the very attempt to write requires that I no longer have a body; and what matters more than myself is the feeling of what I yearn to say, while my awareness keeps stretching toward inspiration… and maybe the sky.

But what's in my room, along with me and all my writing supplies? Pressure from the relentless passage of time, also fear of my looming deadline. And. The. Words. Which. Won't. Come. Out.

By my junior year of college, every one of my papers is a dismal failure. Dr. Grossman, who has become my official Advisor by then, meets with me once each semester. And he offers, offers! to give me a private tutorial for help with my writing.

Dr. Grossman, the most popular professor in the whole English Department and a published poet, he volunteers to give me the honor of an independent study?

Dazzling though the prospect is, somehow, I never dare to schedule this mentoring with him. Instead, I request independent study with somebody who seems more my speed, not an amazing brain, but obviously she must be smart and love poetry. You see, I manage to track down the only female professor in the English Department, Dr. Aileen Ward, renowned as a Keats scholar.

Studying my very favorite poet, Gerard Manley Hopkins, with Dr. Ward? That would be heaven… if she and I could develop one tenth of the rapport I have with Dr. Grossman. Unfortunately, that never happens. Before my final project, Dr. Ward allows me just two meetings, each one as stiff as it is brief. Finally, after reviewing my independent study, she grades me a C.

As for our final tutorial meeting, a meeting that lasts five slow minutes, Dr. Ward fixes me with her brainy blue eyes and sneers, "I certainly hope you never plan to go to graduate school."

Meeting over!

Questing Reader, eventually something does lift my nightmarish, stupefying case of writers' block. I'll tell you about that later. But now it's time to report on a part of college life that matters as least as much as the classes and, even, the writing. You see, I have decided to become a hippie.

CHAPTER 22

The Strangest Reason to Meet Timothy Leary

Maybe pot will help me to find God. After a fine meal in the dining hall I'm sitting in my dorm room, conversing pleasantly with my neuroses, when a girl who lives down the hall invites me over to her room and then, bam! I make a discovery that I've been yearning for, like, forever.

While kids like me sit cross-legged in a big circle, skinny hand-rolled cigarettes are passed around. Although this clockwise rotation is simple enough, and the game doesn't seem hard to play, my heart is beating like that peppy little bongo drum my dad brought home last year.

When your turn comes, you're supposed to take a deep toke on the joint, then hold in the smoke for as long as you can, as if preparing to swim underwater. Two tokes and I'm high, although I continue taking tokes off every single joint offered.

How does it feel, being high? For as long as I can remember, I've felt imprisoned, as if living inside a kind of box, the box of having to be myself, one very limited person, a person *trapped* inside that box, a person stuffed with worries on the inside and on the outside, showing the world her pimples.

Finally being stoned, what changes? Clear as day, I can tell that my box isn't real. Problems that normally feel as solid as the tongue in my mouth... turn whatever-ey. And, thanks to weed, my stoned mind realizes quite decisively that I am *not* that person trapped in a box. Quite rapidly I discover that, in consciousness, I can travel anywhere. Like when looking at the hand of the girl sitting next to me, all I need do is point my eyes at her elbow and then, with the gentlest of whooshes, my mind moves inside hers. Instantly I can know her deeper, better, and soooooo meaningfully, far beyond words.

Next day, all day long, my heart waltzes with the promise of it, my initiation into grass! Finally, I have managed to get stoned, just like Jack Kerouac and all the beatniks and maybe even Aldous Huxley with his Doors of Perception. True, I didn't get stoned deeply enough to find God, but maybe that will happen if I get better at this. Clearly, all I need is practice.

Soon as possible I buy all the necessary supplies: a *nickel bag* (in 1965, that means all the pot you can buy for five dollars, which is quite a lot of money). Then I purchase my own pipe and, most definitely, I buy into a new goal in life, to become a pothead. Annoyingly, this doesn't work out as planned. Altogether I manage to get stoned maybe once, reverently using my brave new weed skills until... what happens exactly during my second, solo, great pot adventure?

I find myself walking inside an enormous wonderland forest, a vast wooded area that has suddenly sprung up on campus — odd that I never saw it before, but all the better! This flower child is ready and eager to become one with actual flowers, except there are no flowers here. Instead, I become one with the rocks, and then start singing in concert with different, individual blades of grass. Soon I'm grooving along with the entire earthly, rainbow-spattered, Perfection Concert of Life. Then, not meaning to do anything acrobatic, I look up at the sky. Helloooooo!

The mere act of aiming eyes upward? This makes my entire head open up, propelling me toward the sky. As in, losing myself in the sky. But soon, as in... frustrating! I mean, man, why can't I keep on going, move all the way up *through* the sky and finally get somewhere?

Except maybe my stuckness is a cosmic message, like I'm supposed to remain here on earth.

Sighing, I decide to demonstrate my obedience by improvising a solemn ritual. This includes hanging something onto a tree branch; hanging all that I have in the world, at the moment; hanging my plastic bag with the pot stash and pipe onto that tree branch. Such a beautiful ceremony, intended to loosen up my brain – so that I can become one with all that is.

Clearly, I must learn more human-type things before I'm allowed to go all the way up to the stars. Later that day, when life shrinks back to grumpy-normal, I realize that all my pot-smoking paraphernalia has vanished. Searching never turns it up, either. Mysteriously I can't even locate that vast forest again. Odd how someplace that big would disappear!

Nonetheless, I'd still have to say that weed is Laura's Great Discovery for her first year of college. Back home for summer vacation, I tell my father and sister all about it. Somehow, I don't think Mom would understand. (Turns out, I'm right.)

Why talk so much to the family at all? Because sophomore year is over and so, once again, I'm back home for summer vacation. That means Mom and Dad and Amy and me, with me feeling totally bored out of my gourd. What a relief that I get a call from my high school friend Donna, inviting me to visit her at college! At Antioch the kids do an unusual work-study arrangement, so she's in school now even though I'm not.

Supportive as always, my parents give me the money for this spur-of-the-moment adventure. Later, that very day, I exchange my family's apartment in Queens for a long, hot ride in Greyhound busses — yes, make that busses plural — because one of them breaks down partway through and must be replaced with a different bus.

Who cares, though? Eventually, I arrive at Donna's college in Yellow Springs, Ohio, and she looks the same as ever: apple-cheeked pretty, with ash blonde hair and merry eyes. Donna shows me around while we talk nonstop, catching up on each other's life stories. Like me, she has been experimenting with a lot of boyfriends and smoking pot — okay, both of these *lots* being way more than I've done, by the sound of it. Her fave is combining sex with getting high, where the guy will say, like, "Where are you, Donna? Come back, Donna."

What, she's hardly in her body, and yet at the very same time, having sex? That's too funny. We giggle as if we were back in high school. College life is just amazing, isn't it?

Suddenly a phone call interrupts our conversation. Uh-oh, it's not just my family checking that I arrived in Ohio safely. My Dad sounds furious, and he quickly gets to the point. There is a problem, a very big problem, a problem that apparently is all my fault. Questing Reader, for background, during the last two weeks of my long sophomore summer, Amy has been at summer camp. From there she just sent me a postcard, which was delivered today. Even though it's addressed to me, a postcard could be read by anyone of course, and when Mom read it, she hit the roof.

Now, over the phone, Dad reads it to me:

"Hi, Laura. Guess what we're doing at camp? Smoking pot. I love it, just like you said I would. Thanks so much for telling me about it. We're out by the water right now, getting high. Camp is groovy!"

My first reaction is to laugh out loud. What a fool she has turned out to be! Guess nobody told her yet about "be discreet." My

Dad agrees that Amy's postcard is funny in a way. "But your mother is unbelievably upset. She wants you to come home immediately."

"But I just got here," I say, indignantly.

"First thing tomorrow, you take that bus home," Dad says, using his angriest voice.

Sighing, I prepare for another long bus ride and then, probably, another long fight with my mother.

Donna understands everything. Also, she agrees with me that Amy's postcard is absolutely hilarious. So we laugh for a while, and then continue to enjoy our visit — which, we now realize, is going to be extremely short. Still, as both of us know, we hippies must learn to be flexible. That's a requirement for being cool.

The very next morning we laugh some more. We hug. Then I carry my hardly-used suitcase onto another bus. This Greyhound bus breaks down again, maybe in the exact same spot for all I know. Highway looks like highway anywhere, right?

Back home, almost immediately, Mom and Dad and I enter into one of those family fights where the word TRAUMATIC could be stamped on our Polaroid photo with a big red rubber stamp. Leading off, Mom demands to know about my pot smoking.

My reply? "Of course, I smoke pot. All the kids at school do."

At first Mom looks horrified, with disgust that seems to drip all the way through her, dripping down from her scowl, dripping down all the way into her ingrown toenails. Next my mother accuses me of becoming addicted.

"That's crazy. I'm not addicted," I tell her.

"You're already addicted to cigarettes," she says, screaming even louder than before.

"I. Am. Not." I yell back. "All I smoke is one lousy pack a day, not like you and Dad, with your 3 ½ packs! Every single day of my life!"

"Laura, you know that I can't help it. Blame those cigarettes," she says, starting to look victim-like in her usual way. "If you're not addicted, prove it. Promise me right now that you'll stop smoking cigarettes. I mean it."

"Okay, okay," I scream. "Are you happy now?"

"No," she snaps back. "I won't be happy until you and Dad drive over to Amy's camp. I mean, you go there right now. Then you tell her from me, she's got to stop smoking that marijuana."

"Like for when, man, forever?"

"That's right. No kidding. So, first thing tomorrow, both you and Ernie. Drive there, very first thing."

Never have I seen my mother so angry. Personally, I think it's a big joke. Smoking pot makes Amy cool. All the kids I know who smoke pot tell me it's safe, only establishment people have made it illegal, and that's because they're so... establishment.

As for stopping the cigarettes, that won't be a problem for me. I never really liked them, I only smoked to look cool and sophisticated. Alone in the car with Dad, he tells me that he's been smoking pot for a long time. He knew about it even before I told him. Then he reminds me that after work sometimes he goes to his favorite nightclub, Birdland. All the cool jazz musicians go there. Between sets, they talk. Blow some weed. Hang out.

Dad drives fast on the highway, the two of us having a great time, as if we're talking and laughing at way more than 60 miles an hour. After a while, Ernie spots some hitchhikers at the side of the road. Back in college, I've done that. Hitchhiking is one of the cool things that people do these days. Once, Zero Mostel's son Josh gave me a ride, and he was sweet.

Now my father is hip to hitchhiking, too? Apparently, since he pulls over and picks up the two hitchhikers. Into the back seats go Evvie and Sally, girls about my age, dressed really cute in hippie clothes. When Dad asks where they're going. they tell him it's a place called Millbrook.

Always ready for adventure, that's my father. When they tell him where Millbrook is, he says, "Sure, that could be on our way." If they don't mind waiting, that is. First he and his daughter must do a short errand at our destination. After that, we'll take them to Millbrook.

As for our original errand, we take care of it quickly enough; locating Amy with no trouble; then explaining in detail why her postcard got her into big trouble with Mom. Dutifully, Dad and I execute the official conversation and extract an official promise from her: No way will she smoke pot ever again — at least not until she leaves home for college.

Mission accomplished, Dad drives Evvie and Sally and me out to Millbrook. The girls explain, it's the home of a man named Timothy Leary. He's a very, very cool man, famous for introducing America to LSD. Once we arrive, what becomes obvious? Millbrook makes Amy's summer camp look tame. Leary runs a kind of camp for grownups, apparently, and we're free to give ourselves a tour.

A mansion more than merely a house, it's unbelievably enormous, with countless rooms that straddle exceptionally long corridors. At the end of one of these, I notice a mirror that has been shattered and glued back together so that a pile of jagged little pieces automatically scramble up your reflection, creating the strangest, chunked-up, Picasso-worthy, reflections of your face.

This reminds me of a book by my favorite writer these days, Herman Hesse. In one of his novels, *Steppenwolf*, the main character sees his life in fragments. That vision brings him big discoveries about God and himself.

And wow, here is a mirror that probably is meant to do the same kind of thing, automatically even, so that you don't have to manage all that work inside your own head.

To say that I'm eager to stare into that mirror for several hours and find Big Truth! Inconveniently I can grab only a few seconds right now, and the mirror doesn't seem to do a thing for me. Sometimes I feel so disgusted with myself.

Despite my disappointing experience with the mirror, I find plenty to observe here at Millbrook. For one thing, everybody speaks very, very slowly. For another, they seem unusually spaced out, even compared to other hippies I've met. As for the great Timothy Leary, what happens when we meet him? Surprisingly, the man seems like a normal person, verging on boring, and not the least bit memorable. For example, he offers us some grapes and after we decline, he wanders away.

Ice cream? Now that I will never pass up. But boring old grapes?

Years later, I tell somebody the story about meeting Timothy Leary. I mention how disappointing it was that all he did was to offer us some grapes. "Are you kidding?" says my friend. "Those grapes are famous. Each one contained a complete acid trip. Do you realize, every single person you met at Millbrook was stoned out of his mind?"

As for me, being oblivious to the real action really there at Millbrook, this place isn't such a big deal, not to me. Mostly this is a sweet summer day, hanging out with my Dad, a day made sweeter by having done my duty regarding my errant little sister.

Admittedly, while there, I do figure out one thing. Some of the people at Millbrook might be a bit strange. For instance, shortly before leaving, while still exploring the property with my Dad, we find a cute little pool. It's neat and square, no longer than three feet along each side. And yet this pool looks extremely deep.

While Dad and I stand there, making small talk with others who are standing at the side of the pool, what happens? A lanky young man ambles over. Without bothering to speak to anyone, this guy composes himself, curling his bare toes around the edge of the pool.

Suddenly, quick as a blink, he springs upward really high, then executes a perfect jackknife into the water, going deep.

After a while, his wet head emerges. Gracefully he climbs out of the pool, moving in a startlingly composed manner, like Mr. Cool. Following that, he turns away from all of us by the pool. He walks away, never uttering a single a word to any of us who have been watching him. Including my father and me: We are staring with rounded eyes and mouths opened wide, in a perfect position for screaming, if needed.

After Mr. Cool moves on to his next athletic feat, or whatever, Dad and I look at each other, simply astounded. Especially since nobody else standing around our pool… appears to consider this dive to be the least bit peculiar.

Personally, I'm creeped out. If that huge dive had been off by even a few inches, Mr. Cool could have given himself a concussion. How do I know?

As a child, I saw that happen once at a regular swimming pool, with a big diving board positioned 10 feet up, perfectly placed for that Olympic-sized pool. Yet somehow a teenage girl in a cute swimsuit missed the water entirely. She passed out on the concrete. I saw doctors take her away in an ambulance. And, for all I know, that jump nearly killed her.

Altogether, I don't mind saying goodbye to Millbrook. As Dad drives us home, we get back to hanging out just the two of us, so very comfortable. That's our usual way of being together. Except this time, we're also laughing and laughing inside. We managed to do exactly what Mom wanted. If she only knew what else we did!

Will we tell her? Of course not. I am learning a lot about *Be Discreet*.

CHAPTER 23

A Shower of Indignation

My first conversation with Donald: I'm in line at the dining hall, hungry for dinner, when a boy taps me on the shoulder. After I turn to face him, this stranger asks me, "Would you like to go out tonight and hear a concert with Jimi Hendrix?"

Quickly I glance at the guy's handsome face, his muscular build, his gorgeously contagious smile and, come to think of it, a very peculiar tee-shirt he's wearing — pastel green with blue stripes, an old-guy shirt that I later learn he has bought from Goodwill (like the rest of his wardrobe). Such an intriguing and sexy stranger has just asked me for a date!

Obviously, what comes next? I tell him, "No." Then turning around, I continue my avid pursuit of dinner. Am I ever famished. Hey, it smells like the cafeteria's serving chicken and broccoli, excellent!

Questing Reader, lest I give the impression that romantic dates of any kind, let alone live concerts with a top musician of the day; just in case you're curious whether such invitations are offered to me on a daily basis, like hot, nourishing food on plastic trays at my dining hall, alas, my answer would have to be, "You kidding?"

In my entire life by now, I've had maybe three official dates. Granted, I'm a college junior and, thus, have expanded my array of failed love relationships to include a philosopher, a poet, and a photographer. None of them took me out on official dates, though. Anyway, heartbreak is standard for college, right? By any definition, my current social life is tremendous, at least when compared with eight years at U.N.I.S., that tiny school with 15 in the graduating class, only 4 of them boys.

Besides, at Brandeis the students are different; all of them seem interesting and, for the most part, they're friendly and smart and articulate. My *Be Discreet* residence counselor, for example: one night she gives a free clarinet concert, accompanied on piano. This woman could have been a professional musician. Listening to her play, I weep, it's that beautiful.

Really, I can't believe my luck, being allowed to attend a school with such talented people. Why did Admissions ever let me in? Undoubtedly a mistake, but will I ever 'fess up? No way.

Campus is gorgeous, with rolling lawns and flowers. Apparently my neighborhood forsythias aren't the only kind of blossoms that can grow outside. Honestly, in my part of Flushing, my only garden-related encounter was reading *Lady Chatterley's Lover*. While here at beautifully landscaped Brandeis, I see my first daffodil, and later an entire hillside of them, daffodils like miniature suns visiting with each other, because where could it be more wonderful for daffodil-suns to visit and talk and talk and talk?

Concerts on campus are fantastic, outdone only by the plays. Granted, they're not *My Fair Lady*, yet these campus plays thrill me as much as anything I've seen on Broadway. As someone who never went to a nightclub or bar before freshman year, I can hardly believe my good luck that Brandeis has Cholmney's, our own coffee house, where you can hang out any night of the week.

Plus, there's a college chorus to join, and even a Camerata where I can sing my favorite choral music of all, by Josquin des Pres and other Renaissance composers. Anything wonderful you might want, I bet you could find it here at college.

Yet what's not so great for me here? Writing papers — as you know by now, Questing Reader. Since switching my major to English Literature, I'm duty bound to write loads of papers. Based on personal experience, I could write a really detailed paper about one thing... writer's block. Except that, ouch, I can't.

What's the big deal if I'm neurotic, though? Around here, who isn't? At Brandeis in the 60's, campus culture is idealistic, psychologically investigatory, politically liberal, and predominantly Jewish; this last part helps me to feel unexpectedly comfortable, since before college I haven't met many Jews.

Other religions might be different. With Judaism you don't have to actively be religious in order to belong. Being Jewish means what? Seems to me, we're really sensitive, usually very messed up, and also big seekers of God. These days, of course, being spiritual also means calling yourself a hippie. To me, being a hippie means wanting to make the world a better place.

It means caring about social justice, like volunteering (which I do, tutoring poor kids in Chelsea). Also, being a hippie means demonstrating in Boston, where I march against the Vietnam War. With all my heart I believe in today's new ideal of "Make love, not war."

Smoking grass fits perfectly with hippie idealism. I'll do whatever it takes to discover the truth about life, to find a way to love every person I meet, and to live with love every single chance I can find.

Hopefully my generation can turn life inside out, bringing what's authentic to the surface instead of hiding what really matters, as so many of our parents have done. Conformity? Here that's either hidden or banished!

We hippies replace that with honesty: Speak your truth and hear the other person's truth. That's the only authentic way to live.

Just like my conversation with that boy who asked me out to hear Jimi Hendrix: Let's get to the point and be real, everyone. The Beatles are singing about our discoveries, so it's a big deal whenever they come out with new records like *Revolver* and later, *Sgt Pepper's Lonely Hearts Club Band*.

Campus conversations move fast, deliciously seasoned with wit. For instance, we're now very aware of *camp*, which is a cool kind of irreverence that's becoming popular. Compare that to when I grew up. What used to be the biggest compliment you could give a person? To call him *sincere*. Well, forget that!

Incidentally, I do start noticing this boy, Donald Davis. Soon I develop the crush to crush all crushes. In his dormitory, a bunch of the kids get together to form an *encounter group*, which is a new craze. Somehow, I'm allowed to become a member of this Ridgewood Group.

Once a week, we do exercises about consciousness, exercises that somebody learned from somebody who knew somebody else who once went to Esalen. (That's a trendy place now, in California.) Trust exercises and deep, intense sharing -- in a way, these shares teach me more than my classes. You see, Questing Reader, our encounter group exercises feel like my ticket to become an adult, a liberated *new* kind of adult.

Whenever we meet in the Ridgewood Group, we'll do a process and then break out into small groups for discussions. Out the corner of my eye, I'll watch what happens with Donald's group.

Soon I notice a pattern. Whichever small group he's in becomes the liveliest one of them all. Donald always makes conversations turn authentic, probably due to being so smart. And funny. And outrageous.

One day when we're talking, Donald mentions that he scored a perfect 800 in his Math SAT. Wow! Far as I'm concerned, this boy is so smart, he could become a college professor. Gradually, we start hanging out together, and "getting physical" too.

Nobody else is like Donald, who describes himself as *a mystic artist soul man*, introducing me to music by Otis Redding. Donald plays music too: both soulful clarinet and saxophone. Incidentally, he does eventually take me to a Jimi Hendrix concert, which I find both uncannily virtuosic and deeply unsettling.

Outrageous Donald makes friends with professors, too: totally opposite to my habitual cowering before anyone who might grade me. Of course, Donald can have deep conversations with anyone, anybody at all. Soon we're invited to dinner at the home of our sociology professor, Sam Wallace. Could anything deliver more sophistication than being served a fantastic dinner for four by his wife, Susan Wallace?

Well, how about this? After we finish the scrumptious brownies and ice cream, Professor Wallace lights up a joint.

A professor who smokes pot with us? I don't think I've ever felt more grown up. Dr. Wallace is one of my most interesting professors, because he earned his Ph.D. by going undercover to research skid row culture. Imagine, for years, he pretended to be an alcoholic, a bum living out on the street. Such a courageous man! Eventually he published a book on all his sociological research.

Donald's fearless way with faculty even helps me to get into an exclusive seminar. For starters, he finds out that Professor Dick

Katz is on loan from Harvard, where he has been working with Timothy Leary (!) and Richard Alpert.

Questing Reader, fast-forward to a huge lecture hall filled with hundreds of students. Each of us writes an essay, explaining why we hope Dr. Katz will choose us to be in his experimental seminar. Only 20 places will be available. Odds are, I'll never get in, that's for sure.

Except that clever Donald arranges for a brief faculty meeting the next week. It's just him and me and Dr. Katz, all three of us chatting away in his office. Despite feeling so shy that I could melt into my plastic chair, soon I'm part of an interesting discussion. A week later, when the seminar roster comes out, I'm on the list — along with Donald. Another member of our seminar is some relative of another Brandeis professor, Dr. Abraham Maslow. Maybe she's his niece? I'm not sure but, definitely, this course in Nonverbal Communication is going to be a big deal.

With Dr. Katz we do Esalen-style exercises, too, but they're better than what we do in the Ridgewood Group. Most of the time we keep silent. After each exercise we debrief. Only then do we talk about what we noticed nonverbally. Life changing!

Instead of a final exam, the whole group stays together at a farmhouse in the country, our own special world together, where we spend four days communicating with each other, only nonverbally. One fellow, who later becomes a professional philosopher, solemnly strips down to his true naked self, but the rest of us manage to keep on our clothes. Whatever! We're a tolerant crew, and not mostly nudists, just trying hard to learn all we can about communication and energy and being.

If only all my classes could be this thrilling! Well, actually, they are. And campus life thrills me, too. By the second semester of my junior year, I'm living in the best dorm on campus and loving life passionately. The Castle is an oddly shaped dormitory that looks like a miniature castle, minus the moat. This oddly-shaped building is divided into quirky little dorm rooms. I share mine with Eda Warren, whose glittery green eyes are framed in black lashes, as though she was destined to become an artist (which she is). Eda is brilliant and also deliciously neurotic.

Unofficially, Donald also lives in our dorm room. He shares my bed more often than he stays at his official residence hall. One Friday night, Donald and I want to plan something fun for the weekend, but what? Ha, inspiration strikes! We take a shower together. Afterward we can get stoned, and then we'll study for an exam.

Soon we're shampooing each other, tucked into a shower stall at the girl's bathroom at my end of the dorm. Oh, we are having such a blast! Granted, this isn't a sexual kind of playtime, more like two big kids bathing together for the first time. Soon I'm in the midst of giving Donald a wondrous shampoo, practically psychedelic from the crazy amount of bubbles. All of a sudden, wham!

With no warning, I hear the door to our floor's bathroom make a loud sound, as if somebody is slamming it open. Next, I hear the sound of a woman wearing high heels. Her righteous steps make a stomping, clickety noise on the linoleum. Then she speaks. Her stern voice blares like a megaphone at a sporting event.

"This is Mrs. Hockenstadt, your residence counselor. Open up that shower curtain. I know you have a man in there."

Uh-oh. Donald and I could be in serious trouble. Frantically I try hiding my boyfriend by pushing my head in front of the blue plastic shower curtain. Meanwhile I use my left hand to pinch the curtain closed beneath my chin.

Simultaneously, my right hand is desperately trying to push Donald back, in the opposite direction of that shower curtain.

"Nobody's here," I holler.

"What? What?" Donald says, thrashing against the curtain with his arms.

"Really, what's the problem?" I continue, innocently. "It's only me in here." Although I'm new to major league lying, now seems like an important time to learn.

Meanwhile, Donald begins flailing his arms around even more forcefully. "What's happening? Who's out there?" he shouts. Soap from the shampoo has gotten into his contact lenses, plus his ears, and so he can't quite hear the insistent voice of my residence counselor.

Well, I can. Mrs. Hockenstadt doesn't believe me, for some reason. Angrily she continues to insist that some man is there with me, hiding right in the shower stall.

As if talking to idiots, she explains that the two of us have made very loud noises, especially all the laughing, until a girl living directly above this bathroom couldn't stand it anymore. That's when so she called Mrs. Hockenstadt to complain.

Throughout this indignant explanation, Donald keeps pushing against my restraining arm until finally he breaks through, poking his head out through the curtain. "Who's there?" he hollers, blinking.

Soon we are wrapped in towels, walking the march of shame in front of Mrs. Hockenstadt. Oh, we are in such big trouble. In the entire history of Brandeis, we are the first couple ever to be caught taking a shower together. Clearly, we have failed dismally at "Be discreet."

What happens in days to come? Apparently, some school administrators want to expel Donald and me. However, university rules dictate that we must be tried by the student government. Mercifully, these kids let us off with a warning to never, ever again do such a stupid thing as to get caught together, taking a shower in a dormitory.

Months later, though, there's more. There's definitely more. When financial aid decisions are announced for the next year, both Donald and I are notified that our senior year scholarships have been cancelled. Financial expulsion? It becomes the talk of the campus. One boy, Bob, comes up to me and offers to hold a campus-wide protest on our behalf.

"What?" I squeak. To me, a protest means demonstrating against something important like stopping the Vietnam War, not whining over a couple of letters from the Financial Aid Office.

Yet, apparently, college demonstration-making is one of many things in life that I don't understand well yet. Insistently Bob explains to me that Brandeis students are itching to protest something, which I ought to know if I followed the news, because of what just happened at Kent State College. April 26, 1968, in Columbus, Ohio! That student demonstration made national news.

According to Bob, this withholding of scholarships, penalizing Donald and me for exercising our freedom to bathe — this might be a perfect cause for a protest. Besides, it just might help us to get our scholarship money back.

Oh, I can easily imagine how much my mother would love watching that on the Evening News.

"Thanks a lot. Really," I tell Bob, "But no."

Over the next week, however, professors Wallace and Grossman go to bat for Donald and me, meeting with school administrators, insisting that we are terrific students, pleading that we shouldn't be de facto expelled. Quietly as a whisper — or hush money being passed under a table — our financial aid is restored; thankfully, our parents never learn about the shower incident.

However, those hot-to-trot protesters on campus soon organize a different kind of demonstration. Weeks after I decline Bob's offer, activists take over an administration building, Ford Hall, occupying it for 11 days in January 1969. Since participating in a protest seems cool, one night I do a sleepover with the other protesters.

Embarrassing but true, I have only the vaguest idea of what exactly we're protesting. Except probably it's The Establishment. Never trust anybody over 30, of course!

Undoubtedly to Bob's delight, this Brandeis protest does make national news. Our college is that kind of place. We have given the world Abbie Hoffman and Angela Davis. Later we'll produce Wayne Dyer, Thomas L. Friedman, and Mitch Albom (who writes a bestseller about one of my sociology professors, Morrie Schwartz). And now, ta da! We Brandeisians are giving the world Ford Hall.

Years later, Dr. Wallace indulges in a protest of his own. I'm told he publishes a book that reveals his sociological findings about a pathologically liberal, self-absorbed, pot-smoking college culture, where he has posed as one of the hippies.

By then, however, Donald and I are married.

CHAPTER 24

Hey Man, Got Change?

What happens during Ernie Rosenbaum's first conversation with my Donald? He and Mom have driven the four-hour trip from New York to visit me at the Castle, celebrating how their elder daughter has just turned twenty years old.

After my dad walks over to a vending machine, buying himself a pack of cigarettes, a college boy approaches. This boy is dressed like a typical hippie: long hair, wrinkled tee shirt, scruffy beard, and he doesn't look or smell as though he has bathed in weeks.

Maybe this young man can't bathe on his own. Evidently, he does know how to speak. "Hey man, do you have change for the vending machine? I want to get some Coke."

Ernie's pockets always jingle with coins. Immediately he pulls out change for a dollar, hands it over to the college kid, and waits to receive a $1 bill back in exchange.

Instead, the boy simply grabs Dad's money, buys himself the can of soda, returns all the change to *his* pocket, and leaves, saying over his shoulder, "Thanks, man."

Astonished, Dad watches. Being a cool guy himself (and not only because he also wears a beard), he chuckles inwardly at the silly kid. Then Ernie takes his new pack of Pall Malls and returns to his daughter's dorm room. Except now he sees a boy in this room; that very same boy, who's nearly finished with his ill-gotten can of Coca Cola; that grungy, arrogant boy; a boy who's no longer simply somebody to chuckle over, either. Because this boy has arrived in the dorm room belonging to Ernie's own daughter, where she sits next to him comfortably. On. Her. Bed.

Ernie's eyes turn next toward Sue, who sits awkwardly on a chair, much as he left her. Except that he thought she was in shock even before he went for the cigarettes.

Already weirded out by the sight of this bizarre excuse for a college dormitory, by now Sue has gone way deeper into shock. Although she's sometimes seen hippie boys on TV, and even passed some of them on the street, never before has she been so close to one.

I look first at Dad, then at Mom, taking it all in. Immediately I ignore it all, having perfected this art years ago.

Moving right along, I declare in a voice of absolute crush, "Mom, Dad, I want you to meet Donald Davis. We're living together."

Okay, so I haven't told my folks about him before, not a word, not once. Honestly, calling or writing to one's parents? That doesn't happen much to people like me.

This is college and, sure, I love them, but I'm all grown up by now. Besides, they're over 30, so how can I possibly trust them? The way I see it, minimal communication with parents is practically *my duty* now that I'm a hippie.

Questing Reader, let's leave aside the thought of my horrified mother, having to drive back from Brandeis a second time... on this occasion undoubtedly alternating her piteous sobs with screams of rage at this idiotic daughter of hers.

As for me? Post-visit, I fling away from my conscience any thoughts of my father, who has made it his duty to do everything in his power to indulge his self-centered daughter. As if it weren't enough to deal with his high-maintenance wife -- sigh!

Moving right along, Questing Reader, I'll continue to share with you what matters most to me at this time in my life. Unfortunately, this includes precious little gratitude toward, or closeness to, my parents.

What does matter to me, concluding my junior year? I fall in love, a bigger love even than my adoration of Donald.

PART FIVE. Questing

Chapter 25

Inside Strawberry Jello

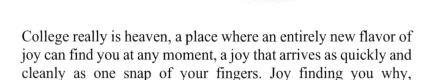

College really is heaven, a place where an entirely new flavor of joy can find you at any moment, a joy that arrives as quickly and cleanly as one snap of your fingers. Joy finding you why, exactly? Simply because you choose to enter a classroom.

You see, Questing Reader, one of my coolest professors -- Dr. Larry Rosenberg – has organized a special evening seminar with a friend of his, one of the hippie Harvard professors like Timothy Leary (from Millbrook) and Dick Katz (who was my professor for Nonverbal Communication).

Evidently this third guy, also a former leader of the Harvard Psilocybin Project, may be the most remarkable free spirit of all. Once a tenured professor, Richard Alpert has forsaken his ivory tower to turn spiritual pilgrim, traveling to India and studying with a guru.

Now he's back to tell us all about it. Before the evening seminar, all I've learned for sure is that Dr. Alpert recently returned from India, having given himself a new name, a spiritual name, and a name that's pretty darned different from Richie or Rick or Dickie. His name is Baba Ram Dass!

Still, I guess the Harvard in him must be coming out now, since tonight he's giving one of his very first public talks since his past life as a psych professor. Ram Dass will speak about something entirely different from psychology. What's the rumor? The famous professor has returned from India as a changed man, a man in spiritual Enlightenment.

That's all Donald and I know about him, but it's a pleasant spring evening, the seminar is free, and we know that sociology professor Dr. Rosenberg is cool. We're game to hang out with this unusual visitor.

In the normal way, we enter a small classroom and take seats among a half-dozen students already there. At the front of this classroom, Professor Rosenberg instantly commands attention, just by his usual presence: a scholar's brilliance spiked with childlike curiosity. Next to him sits a second man who looks really smart, only this one also looks thin, in the strangest, hardly-there way.

He must be Ram Dass. And he proceeds to do *what*? Unlike any professor I've ever seen, this stranger begins his talk by closing his eyes. Gazing inward? Contemplating his navel in search of ancient lint? So far, I'm not into taking this guy too seriously.

Smiling gently, then, in a manner that seems both mysterious and self-satisfied, Ram Dass proceeds to open his eyes. Immediately he begins to check out every member of the audience, gazing at each of us individually, a kind of taking turns while he silently introduces himself to our souls.

Not odd to me, exactly, this reminds me a bit of the far-out exercises at the Ridgewood Group and, definitely, my groovy classes with Dr. Katz. Fascinated, I feel how something distinctly nonverbal is happening here. Moreover, this mysterious new something is going to be absolutely thrilling. This I can tell already.

Uncharacteristically silent, we chatty college kids watch Ram Dass while he's watching us, one at a time. Some he stares at longer than others.

When my turn comes, I can't wait to boldly stare right back at him. Whoosh! I'm pulled into a new kind of silence, like a kind of amusement park ride, a ride that feels as if I'm physically zooming upward, riding all the way to the top of my Consciousness Ferris Wheel, and then falling upward still further, until I'm out of my seat entirely, transported into an entirely different dimension.

Although new to me as Laura, somehow this deep, silent space feels totally familiar, as does the way I'm not in my body at all, and yet this disembodied version of me feels more like True-Me than the girl in her slouchy jeans and green sweater.

This trip has nothing like the vibe of a drug high, either. For one thing, Ram Dass is right there with me in the space, his eyes wide open, calm and steady. Also, it feels to me as if I'm traveling in the direction of Home, not quite there, but I'm definitely moving in The Direction.

Next, it dawns upon me that this space with Ram Dass and me is suffused with a bright astral light. (Astral light? What the heck does that mean? Yet somehow that strange name pops into my head as a way to describe the experience. *Astral.*)

This astral light is red, like when you make strawberry Jello and keep diluting the mix with water. Rapturously I'm flying — yes, flying — within this alluring red light.

I'm flying toward Ram Dass with all my heart and soul. His energy pulls me like a magnet. Closer and closer to him I'm flying now, singing inside with the most joyful feeling of Going Home.

No reservations do I feel. I'm totally ready to merge with this man who reminds me of Home. How much I want to join with him in that astral, gigantic, weightless, joyful, unlimited space that somehow feels so strangely familiar.

Ram Dass lives always in this bright red world. It's the main place he lives, I just know it. So I cry, inwardly, like a screaming kind of prayer:

Let me live there, too.

Inches from his body now, I'm throbbing with this urgent desire as if it were some new kind of heartbeat, a heartbeat that fits into my totally-natural-feeling body of light.

NO!

The word sounds within me like a command, that one word firing as loud as a gunshot, a wholly unexpected word that comes from someone else, neither Ram Dass nor me. Immediately I slam back into my body, still seated on a white chair made of hard molded plastic.

Full of wonderment, I look over at Donald and meet his eyes. Sitting to my left, he's already had his carnival ride with Ram Dass, and now through one look we agree. This evening is going to change everything, and we're thrilled to be sharing this amazing experience together.

Hour after hour, Ram Dass regales his eager audience with teaching tales, anecdotes pulled from his life; like how he took acid with Leary but wanted a more natural high; like how, as college professor Alpert, he then went to India, searching far and wide until he found an Enlightened guru.

And about this guru, we hear one amazing story after another; most notably how the guru drank poison just to prove to his students how even poison can't hurt an Enlightened man because he can do anything. At one point, Ram Dass sings a sacred chant. It's the sweetest singing I've ever heard, by far, and not just better than all the gorgeous music my father used to play from his record collection. This singing is heavenly, reminding me of all my best spiritual seeking.

> ➢ Like those times in high school when I read haiku by the Japanese mystic Basho.
> ➢ Or when I was liberated by the *sprung rhythms* in poems by the Jesuit priest Gerard Manley Hopkins.
> ➢ Better than the bliss I felt when I sang polyphonic masses by Josquin des Prez.
> ➢ And, as an even more recent discovery, how I felt when reading a book that mysteriously landed in my dorm room this year, a book of wisdom from a long-ago spiritual teacher named Meister Eckhart.

Adding up all these experiences and taking them further, that's what happens while I listen to the sublime chanting from Baba Ram Dass.

Next, it's Q&A, not that we seminar students have many questions to ask this time. Seems to me, it's as if every soul in that room has been wrapped in silence.

Questing Reader, just imagine regular people being spiritually gift-wrapped, our own souls turned into presents that we're giving back to God: each of us seamlessly wrapped in shiny paper, a wrapping paper with colors more beautiful than those seen on earth, and ineffable as the huge night sky.

Somebody in the audience asks Ram Dass, "What's your opinion of Maharishi Mahesh Yogi?"

All of us recognize that name. He's an Indian guru, different from the one Ram Dass studied with. Recently the Maharishi has become famous for teaching the Beatles his technique called Transcendental Meditation, TM.

"TM will get you There," Ram Dass says.

Then he adds, "Personally, I'm not a fan of Maharishi. He lies to people. For example, he says that his technique is for householders instead of monks. Also, he says that what he teaches is not a religion. None of this is true."

"Wow," I think! "Impressive about the 'Get you There' part."

CHAPTER 26

Live That

On this bright October day, while I'm walking to class, worries are hamster-wheeling around in my head. It's my senior year now, my last fall at Brandeis. What will I do after graduation?

I have no idea, except that more than anything I would still love to become a poet. Being no Jennifer Cassetari, I haven't investigated well it pays, being a Full-Time Poetess.

Yet I do have a hunch, an unsettling and distinctly practical hunch, along the lines of a financial horror movie. Luckily, classes are the perfect distraction from my practical fears, classes like the one I'm walking to now, a delectable class on American Literature.

For sure, I made the right choice, majoring in literature. How can I worry about anything while in the presence of such great writers? Any little worries of mine are vanquished completely by professors who make the words of great literature… come more alive than ever.

My teacher for this next class, Dr. Swaggart, is that kind of professor. Handsome and witty, he speaks with a voice of authority, like all my Brandeis professors. Every word sounds as clear as a bell, ringing out ideas that startle me more awake.

Of course, it's startling, every class. Who can listen to bells of knowledge like that and, inside, *not* go Boing-Boing-Boing? Settled into my seat in the heaven called *classroom*, I'm engrossed in every bit of bell ringing from Swaggart; as usual, he's pulling great big meanings out of tiny little sentences, immortal sentences written so long ago.

In this particular class, we're studying sentences that were quill-penned by Jonathan Edwards, a fiery preacher whose sermons were so elegant, scholars have promoted them to the category of Great Literature.

Right in this moment, Swaggart has begun reading the best-known sermon by Edwards, *Sinners in the Hands of an Angry God*. As my professor intones the words, an entirely unexpected question asks itself quietly, unexpectedly forming these words inside my head: *What is Jesus really like, anyway?*

This causes something in my brain to click over, like a tumbler turning inside a lock. Instantly, something opens up within me, like a safe door whose lock has been picked, causing that door to swing wide open.

Automatically, in awareness, I'm opening up wide, opening up every particle of me, until I open up so wide that my body no longer contains me at all.

> ➤ And this doesn't involve being pulled out of myself by Baba Ram Dass or by anyone else.
> ➤ Nobody is pulling. Instead, God is being.
> ➤ And I'm simply back to myself as one cozy little part of God.

Finally! No longer am I trapped in the body of Laura, with her neurotic little parade of worries. Instead, I'm a buzzing, vibrating silence. It waves from within itself, like the ocean roar at the beach. *I am That. I have always been That.*

That is in everything. Looking down from the ceiling, I see the top of Laura's head along with the heads of all the students, and also Dr. Swaggart's head. Meanwhile, I hear That. It is singing inside each one of us.

Come to think of it, time isn't working in the usual way. There is only a NOW. Gently, amid the waves of bliss in that NOW, one single thought occurs to me. "I'm having an experience."

Uh-oh, wrong thought. Could I take that back? Instantly, I'm slammed back in my body, squished down into arms and legs and other ridiculous body parts; no doubt about it, I'm back to humdrum human business as usual.

Meanwhile Dr. Swaggart continues talking about Jonathan Edwards. I guess. Usually, I pay total attention in every class. Now all I have is a slightly dizzy attention. It keeps jerking back to what has just happened to me.

Clearly this is the most important experience of my life. So forget worrying about what I must *do* when I grow up! All that matters is what I will *be*. I must become That.

Live That.

Feel That.

Feel one with That always.

How could there ever be any other purpose to my life? After Swaggart's class ends, I walk up the hill toward my next class. Clutching my green book bag, I'm dreamlike yet determined. How can I get back to That? Who would be a good person to ask?

Seems like, all I need do is to ask any of the other kids for advice. Probably all of them know how to become That. Probably they have experiences like the one I just had, only for them it's every single day of their lives; maybe starting off with their normal-type births, so this biggest secret of life that I've just discovered has always been completely obvious to them, so obvious to everybody else that nobody ever bothered to mention it in my hearing.

Finally, someone I recognize comes down the hill. It's Jonathan Miller, a friendly boy I've spoken to a few times. Granted, we're not exactly friends. Yet he's a smart guy, and nice. I take a chance and ask him, quickly summarizing what has just happened. Then I conclude, "Jonathan, do you know how I can get back to That?"

Staring into Jonathan's eyes, demanding an answer, I trust him to tell me. Sure, he's a near stranger, but I'm asking such a simple question, really. Smiling, he pulls out something that he's been carrying, a bulky something tucked under his right arm. Turns out, it's a small stack of posters. Jonathan pulls out one to show me.

It's a typical black-and-white poster, advertising some kind of event on campus. I've seen plenty of them before, with **WHAT**, **WHEN**, and **WHERE** printed in big black letters. Only this poster looks a bit different, since mostly it shows a huge close-up of a man, a big-faced man with a mysterious smile, and a beard that makes him look wise, and black eyes that look like tunnels into forever.

Jonathan points at the man in the poster. "This is Maharishi Mahesh Yogi. What you are talking about, he lives like that all the time. He teaches something called Transcendental Meditation."

That name sounds familiar, although I can't quite place it. Jonathan continues, "It just so happens that today I'm putting up posters for the first-ever TM event at Brandeis. We're having a free Introductory Lecture. "Why don't you come? I think TM could be the answer to what you're looking for. It can get you There."

CHAPTER 27

Initiation

Two weeks later, I've been interviewed by an initiator fresh from India, and he has agreed to teach me. Just like a magic wish granted in some fairy tale, right now, I'm in my *Initiation Room.*

Technically, it's an upstairs bedroom at the Cambridge TM Center, where an everyday dresser has been pressed into service for a special ceremony.

Now this dresser is covered with a white polyblend bed sheet; with a couple of books piled up beneath the sheet to make some kind of religious altar. Quite some picture stands on top. It's the framed portrait of a man who looks unlike anyone I've ever seen before.

He must be Maharishi's own guru. Why would his picture be here, not Maharishi's?

That's just the start of my questions. Such as wondering about the robe flowingly worn by this Indian gentleman. His robe looks like silk, colored a faded orange, which seems like an odd outfit to wear. Maybe an Indian monk's kind of uniform? And what's with his necklace of flowers? Maybe that part is just for special occasions?

Look, Questing Reader, I'm used to dressing down, hippie style. Isn't a monk supposed to be extra-cool? Why would this one dress up more than me?

Yet these baffling details hardly matter, given the impact of this renunciate's face, with blissful eyes like an alien traveler to earth, eyes that remind me of hollowed-out holes in his head, eyes looking out in every direction, looking everywhere at once — except for being not especially interested in seeing what's directly in front of him.

Clearly, there's no time for my silly questions about this Indian man. Before the mysterious altar stands my initiator, Terry Gustafson, a perfectly nice, quiet-looking guy.

Only later do I learn he's famously included in a song by his Teacher Training buddies in India, the Beatles. In their song *Get Back,* lyrics about him include, "Jo-Jo was a man who thought he was a loner."

On this Saturday morning, I know that I'm about to have an "initiation." What has Terry told me to expect? Nothing like this upstairs bedroom tricked out with a religious-type altar!

Instead, Terry has told me this, "As your Initiator, I will perform a ceremony. If you like ceremonies, you'll enjoy this one, since it will be colorful and have flowers and pieces of fruit. If you *don't* like ceremonies, you'll be glad to know that this one is short."

By the time I stand in this room, I have attended two TM talks at my college. After the Introductory Lecture, I eagerly participated in an official Preparatory Lecture that supposedly aimed at getting me ready for this scene.

Except, far as I'm concerned, this place might be weirder than Millbrook! Admittedly, some parts of my two required lectures made sense, like the firm requirement of "No smoking pot for at least 15 days before learning TM." What other preparation have I received?

I sat through a load of promises about full use of my mental potential, perfect health, ideal social relationships (Weird!), and helping to create world peace – all of this, supposedly, if I'd just do 20 minutes of TM in the a.m. and p.m.

And oh yes, "It's not a religion!"

Now, as I stand next to Terry, before that funky altar, what occurs to me? Probably there's a lot that I haven't been told.

Meanwhile, my initiator sings softly in a foreign language, moving around little brass dishes that look like a tea party set belonging to an Indian child. The room smells funny, probably from a burning stick of sandalwood incense.

Most impressively, to me, I can hear the room buzzing in that special way I am learning to associate with Transcendental Meditation, a high-pitched buzzing that feels to me like my favorite part of my very favorite Christmas carol.

Glory to God

In the highest:

Oh, come, let us adore Him

Terry's mysterious song takes a much longer time than *Oh, Come, All Ye Faithful*. Meanwhile, I'm looking around but not seeing much -- understandably, really, since my heart is pounding like maracas. I can't help feeling like I'm in the presence of something big, as if being welcomed into Guru Dev's spiritual family.

But here's the crazy part. It doesn't feel like *my* family. It feels like the *wrong* family, a perfectly nice group of spiritual masters and such, but not the spiritual family I belong to.

This uncanny feeling of wrongness makes no sense whatsoever, but rationality doesn't change how I feel. To comfort myself, I replay the cosmic coincidence of meeting Jonathan Miller with his *first time on campus meditation posters*, which is as close as I'll ever get to having the Cosmic Pointer Finger of God send me a clear message like, "Go and learn TM."

Surely, I'd best conquer my jitters and act like a big girl. Eventually Terry kneels down and motions for me to do the same. Then he turns to me and repeats a meaningless sound called a *mantra*.

After I manage to pronounce it okay, we get up, go sit on our chairs, and I practice what to do with my mantra. Clumsy though I feel, apparently Terry is satisfied that I'm doing okay.

During the lecture given by Terry and the other initiator, Colin Harrison, I've been well prepared for the technical parts of this initiation. I understand that Maharishi's technique, TM, is a kind of "backwards-thinking yoga," leading you to the source of thought.

Initiation includes *getting* a mantra, but the technique — your way of *using* that mantra — matters at least as much as receiving your special sound. After a few short practice periods with Terry, he leads wobbly, confused little me out the bedroom door.

Immediately a helper ushers me to a different room where I sit on a folding chair and start meditating some more.

Behind my closed eyes, something mysterious is happening, for sure. At times, I'm tasting a delicious new kind of space. Other times, I feel like an idiot. Often, emotions of panic rush through me, especially that strange feeling of being in the company of a family that doesn't belong to me.

"Slowly open your eyes," whispers a new helper who comes out of nowhere. Geesh, do I jump!

This latest smiling helper acts as though dealing with startled, shocked people is what she does all day long, every single initiation day at the TM center.

Serenely she leads me to a different room where I fill out a form, answering questions about my first time with the new technique.

As an aspiring writer, I feel encouraged to complain elaborately about how I wasn't prepared enough for the initiation and how I keep having a weird feeling of *wrong family*. Back in the room with Terry, he quickly scans my long essay and sighs. "Are you sure it has been 15 days?" he asks wearily.

"Of course, I haven't smoked pot for 15 days," I snap back at him. "I haven't smoked it for ages."

"Then, you're unstressing a lot, that's all," Terry says. "I don't have time to explain all this to you now, but you do know that we have three group meetings to come. Soon you will understand why you had these feelings. They don't matter at all. Come to our meeting tomorrow and we'll talk further, okay?"

"Not okay, not really," that's how I feel. However, it's clear that my face time with Terry is up. Surely it would be ungrateful to pester this busy young meditation executive.

Back home, I compare notes with Donald, who liked his initiation just fine. During his ceremony, he clairvoyantly saw a whole parade of teachers enter the room, full color, in their spirit bodies, leading off with the guy in the picture, Guru Dev.

That my Donald had such an amazing experience becomes one more reason for me to love him. In TM talk, "He is very highly evolved."

Weeks, then months, into my new life as a TMer, wow! I learn many new ways to talk besides calling people *evolved*. For example, there's *unstressing*. This term that Terry has used on me, what does it mean? How meditation moves out garbage inside of you.

"During meditation, you can feel terrible, but once stress is gone, it is gone for good. When all your stress is gone, you will be Enlightened."

We're all promised that we can have the big cosmic prize. If we meditate faithfully, all of us will be Enlightened in 5-8 years.

I promise myself to never, ever, miss meditation. As for results, the main improvement I notice is how my sense of smell comes roaring and sniffing its way back into my life.

Has my nose had been damaged by stress? Apparently so. Yet, miraculously, I have begun to notice all sorts of fascinating odors.

Granted, I'll never be as smell-iciously talented as my sister Amy, with her uncanny ability to describe and remember fragrances; by comparison with Amy, Marcel Proust would appear insensitive. No need to compete with them, though; it's enough for me to smell the snow, and to smell spring when that arrives.

Thanks so much, Maharishi, for helping me to use my full smelling potential. I can't fully believe in the possibility of spiritual Enlightenment for me, but as consolation prizes go, it's pretty thrilling to realize that I have won by a nose.

CHAPTER 28

Writing and Rounding

Being an English major at Brandeis requires writing lots of long papers which, to me, means just one thing, agony.

The devastating process begins with dread, followed by much pacing, then even smaller-stepped pacing, hamster-like steps near my desk; next follows a great deal of seated pencil chewing (I've tried chewing pens too, but that hurts); followed by countless procrastination hours spent hanging out with other students.

Meanwhile, in the back of my mind, when not writing... I'm straining to figure out what I'll write later. Always the deadline for my assignment comes too soon. Like it or not, I'll wind up pulling an all-nighter, grinding out paragraphs as if extruding them directly from my brain.

Then, a week after submitting my messy typewritten sheets of paper, I'll receive something back in return: a sad, limp grade, usually a C.

Unsurprisingly, by my last semester of college, this hard-working student has garnered only one A, which I received for my course in Nonverbal Communication.

But now this English major is also a meditator and, apparently, this changes something. Assigned five long final papers, I simply go write them, no sweat. Amazingly, every single one receives an A. My last semester of college and finally I'm getting decent grades!

Celebrating my final report card, where I've made Dean's List for the first and only time, I take a few minutes to consider what, exactly, I've done differently. Immediately I'm struck by what I *haven't* done.

All of a sudden, aha! What changed this semester is how I did none of my usual stalling, felt none of my typical anguish. Instead, after being given each assignment, I sat down at my desk and wrote the paper.

Pondering this more deeply, I wonder, is this because TM is taking away my stress? Maybe, but there's got to be something more personal about what has changed for me. Something personal, akin to freeing up my stifled nose to go ahead and smell whatever I like. Writing these latest papers, what was I doing differently?

Wow! With a gigantic rush of gratitude, I get it. This time, when writing I paid attention only to what interested me: Writing and discovering all at the same time, reminiscent of a great quote from Robert Frost that I saw once, "No surprise for the writer, no surprise for the reader."

Understanding what has moved out writer's block for me, I make my own personal Writer's Declaration of Independence.

From now on, I'm allowed to be interested in things.

Just because I'm interested, no other reason.

Whenever I'm going to write something, I'm going to please myself, and write what interests me.

Not what I think should interest me. Nor what I think would impress anyone else.

While writing, I'll live and let live. Which means that I'll finally allow my own writing to live.

Perhaps this insight is a sign that I've begun using more of my mental potential. As for all the other results that I've been promised by now, who knows if meditation will ever make them come true?

Despite my skepticism, that writing breakthrough does impress me, so I pay attention when a friend tells me about an upcoming *TM Residence Course*, a special weekend retreat designed to move you extra-fast toward Enlightenment.

Somehow Donald and I find the money, allowing us to attend the course, which is held at a hotel in Asbury Park, New Jersey. First thing after registration, we move into small classrooms in order to learn yoga asanas, plus a breathing exercise called *pranayama*.

Yoga! Both ancient, exotic, and coming from India: three superb recommendations, far as I'm concerned. And who teaches yoga in my small group? Prudy Bruns, sister to Mia Farrow, the actress; and their mother is Maureen O'Hara, also a famous actress.

Even Prudy is kind of famous, I learn later this weekend. Why famous? Because her training with Maharishi in India included the Beatles, and they wrote a song about her, "Dear Prudence."

Anyway, Prudy is an encouraging teacher, her voice flowing like a clear stream, gently moving in the sunshine. Patiently she corrects how I do each asana. I need a lot of correcting, since I find all of them weirdly hard to learn. At one point, while I'm practicing a bend-over, Prudy stares at me with a horrified expression and blurts out, "For heaven's sake, hold in your stomach!"

Then she proceeds to look even more horrified... at what just popped out of her mouth. Not that I blame her. I'm resigned to the fact that my stomach muscles are hopelessly flabby. Except for that one spontaneous outburst, Prudence proceeds to act just like all the other initiators at our residence course: gliding around all weekend, amazingly peaceful and practically dewy, as though freshly dunked in bliss.

Next comes a meeting led by Maharishi's top initiator in America, Jerry Jarvis, who will be teaching all the group meetings at our residence course.

On stage in the auditorium, Jerry's brainy way of speaking wins me over immediately, and so does his huge, round face, which seems shinier than any other face I've seen; not in a greasy way but more from some kind of inner radiance, a mysterious glow that I can see but also not see.

Definitely, Jerry Jarvis inspires me with every word. Previewing what we'll do this weekend, right in our first group meeting, he announces that we'll devote all our other residence course meetings to deep knowledge about *higher states of consciousness.* Golly!

Also, he explains the special thing that we're allowed to do only on residence courses: *Rounding.* This means something Maharishi invented to help us evolve extra fast.

Here's how rounding works. You do one 20-minute meditation, followed by one set of yoga asanas, plus five minutes of our breathing technique. All that equals One Round. Like in the Beatles song *Dear Prudence*, there's a chorus about that, "Look around, *round.*" So now I know the inside story of what that lyric means!

At the prospect of "going deep into matters of spiritual evolution," I can't wait.

Soon as Jerry's Saturday afternoon lecture is over, I want to disappear quickly, take the elevator up to my hotel room, so I can quietly ponder all the new possibilities I've just been given.

Evidently, my desire for quiet is the exception in this place. Seems like just about everybody else in our group wants to meet Jerry personally and shake his hand.

Understandably so. He's obviously blissful, and also probably the first person in Enlightenment that any of us has ever met, unless we studied personally with Maharishi. Never would I stoop to such obvious tactics. Why not? Because I'm not desperate for bliss. Okay, I am desperate, in private. But in public, I have my pride. No way am I going to beg for this big TM celebrity to single me out, shake my hand, and slather me with darshan.

Darshan, I've been informed by one of the kids on the course, means what happens to a meditator by physically being in the presence of somebody like Jerry, because he can make his Enlightenment rub off on you. Yes, there's an actual word for what, deep down, I'd been hoping might happen. "Yes," I think to myself like a modern-day Oliver Twist, "Please, sir, I want some more darshan."

Only I wonder, is darshan really what these excited course participants want? Or are they more like rock star groupies, mobbing the Beatles? Because this Jerry guy has grown very close to Maharishi, serving as the great guru's right-hand man in America. Turning up my nose in disdain, I exit the lecture hall and rush toward the elevator.

Clearly, I am no groupie. I will bypass the entire, pathetic, crowd. Except that, suddenly, the swarming mass of 200 meditators shifts direction, pushing this way and that, until I slam butt-to-butt — hard! — against someone. Turning around to meet the person attached to this butt, I behold the round and radiant face of... Maharishi's righthand man.

"Why, hello," he says. "My name is Jerry Jarvis. Who are you?"

CHAPTER 29

Marriage, then Microphone

Will I marry Donald? It seems like the thing to do. When we two go back to Queens to visit my parents, I casually mention that we're considering marriage. No asking advice from my parents, of course, which would be so uncool, and aren't we living in the 60s?

In response my father gives Donald a gift, at first, this looks like a cool gift in its way. Dad has bought a forerunner of Rubik's Cube, a classy puzzle from Denmark, intricately fashioned from delicate pieces of polished blonde wood.

Altogether Dad has purchased two of these Danish puzzles. One is shaped like a cube, while the other is spherical. After letting Donald see each puzzle, Dad pulls apart the wooden *cube*, dumping the once-interlocking pieces into a large plastic bag.

Once all these pieces fall into the bag, Dad opens the wooden *sphere* and does the very same thing, tossing this second set of pieces into the same plastic bag. Finally, he proceeds to give the huge mess of puzzle pieces a great big shake.

Completing his symbolic gesture, Dad hands the bag to Donald, saying, "When you can put both of these puzzles together, only then, will I give you my blessing to marry my daughter."

Such a prankster, that father of mine, since even one of those puzzles would be hard to solve on its own. By mixing both puzzles together, he is creating one gigantic headache. Ruining two perfectly good puzzles until they're not going to be any fun at all!

Indignant at being given this insulting present, what's the first thing that Donald and I do, soon as we return to our apartment in Boston? We throw that insulting gift straight into the trash. Sometimes I feel sorry for myself, having parents who just don't understand my one and only love relationship.

Why doesn't my father like Donald? Maybe because, while we were staying at my parents' apartment, behind the bedroom door, the two of us would have a loud fight every single day.

Though, if my parents and sister could hear it, they never said a word. Maybe the yelling wasn't loud at all. Maybe that's only how it felt to me.

Besides, if they had asked about the fights, I would have explained it to them. I'm convinced that all the fighting will help me to heal the man I love.

You see, Questing Reader, Donald has told me how he grew up in poverty, with an invalid mother and an angry breadwinner father whose job was to work at a horrible factory where all he did at work, for decades, was to load heavy cartons of equipment onto trucks.

Even worse, Donald's parents hated each other, barely speaking unless absolutely necessary. Equally bad was their crowded house in the slums, which is where Donald and his sister grew up. Apparently, Donald's family became the only white family that didn't move elsewhere. After the neighborhood started turning black, Donald's family couldn't afford to move.

Just how bad was it, growing up in this poorest part of Providence, Rhode Island? During high school gym class, Donald's teacher wouldn't even let the boys exercise, because very likely they'd fight, and maybe even start a riot.

Questing Reader, can you imagine, being a teenager who's forced to sit on the floor every gym class, and for the entire period? And if the kids started to fidget, even a little, their strict teacher would bellow, "Gentlemen, sit on your numbers."

Granted, Donald seldom tells me stories like this one. Still, he's described enough about his childhood for me to understand how nightmarish it was. Far as I'm concerned, if he needs to fight every single day, pulling me into a loud screaming fight, that's because he needs help to get over that terrible childhood. The least I can do is to let him yell a little.

Soon after that visit with my family in Flushing, we adorable bickerers do decide to get married. Where or how? We haven't a clue, not until I confide in Dr. Grossman that we plan to marry somehow. Immediately, he offers to host our very small wedding at his home in nearby Lexington, Massachusetts.

The most popular professor in the whole English Department is so kind to us, he even finds us a rabbi to officiate at the wedding. Then Dr. Grossman helps us to meet this renowned rabbi by inviting him, along with Donald and me, to his home for dinner, a delicious meal cooked by his beautiful wife Judith. Then follows a glorious Friday night Sabbath that I will never forget.

Such a mystic this rabbi is, it's almost like being with Ram Dass. If Donald and I were to stay in the Boston area, I might even study with this rabbi, he's so amazing.

All our plans fall into place beautifully, now that we have a place for the wedding and even a rabbi. Both of our families agree to come and, somehow, I even find the perfect wedding dress, find it so easily, and it's on sale for some reason.

Questing Reader, imagine a lovely skirt from Marimekko (a Danish company whose clothes are very popular now); a long skirt decorated with elegantly ragged vertical stripes of varying widths, stripes proclaiming my free spirit in brilliant shades of orange, yellow, and bright pink.

Adorning my upper body is a perfect wedding blouse, in sunburst yellow. Amazingly I've also found the perfect earrings to go with my outfit: round earrings, big and dangly; repeating the themes of orange, yellow, and pink — not quite matching, but who cares? The *idea* of matching will have to be good enough.

Which shoes will I dye to match my wedding gown? None. For years I've gone barefoot, except in the snow; why should my wedding be any different?

Before getting all wedding-dolled up, I cook blintzes, because this wedding is to be self-catered. And since this is to be a Jewish wedding, I consult a cookbook which teaches me how to make my first blintzes. No nerves on the morning of our wedding. I'm busy cooking blintzes: some blueberry, others cheese. Yum!

We might not really need 100+ blintzes because it's a very intimate gathering, just Donald's parents and sister, plus my parents and sister, plus that rabbi. And hosting it all are my bespectacled, wise, old professor and his gracious, pink-cheeked wife, Judith.

Our wedding ceremony, if not amazing and mystical like that recent Sabbath, that official wedding goes smoothly enough. Donald's family meets mine smoothly. Everybody eats plenty of blintzes. Most memorable to me is how, at the appropriate moment during the ceremony, Donald smashes a glass with one deft stomp. How I love him! And now we are married forever, happily ever after.

My name has changed now. It's Laura Sue Davis. Cute initials, although I really don't plan to be taking LSD. (Giggle.) What I do plan for is having a most amazing honeymoon.

You see, Questing Reader, as luck would have it, Maharishi is coming to America, giving his second Teacher Training Course ever, his TTC Part One.

Thus, just two weeks into the marriage of Donald and Laura, our unconventional honeymoon begins... in the form of a month-long TM Teacher Training Course at Poland Springs, Maine.

Finally, I'm going to meet Maharishi, whose glowy face has been printed on everything from Intro Lecture posters to the lovely photographs sold at the TM Center. Indian gurus provide their pictures, I'm told, as a favor to their followers, helping you to keep your sacred teacher's image right in your meditation room. Supposedly, looking into the guru's eyes can bring you darshan every time.

Meeting Maharishi in person, at our first course lecture is a gigantic thrill, an other-worldly kind of thrill. Donald and I are seated toward the back of an enormous lecture hall, along with thousands of eager course participants. Quietly, who walks onto the stage? Just a smallish man in a white silk dhoti.

Only this man is accompanied by Jerry Jarvis (wearing a business suit), plus some Indian guys (clad in white robes). Everybody in the audience rises, like giving a standing ovation without the applause. Is this how you're supposed to treat a guru?

For sure, Maharishi Mahesh Yogi is a big deal spiritual teacher. On the stage, he's shiningly front and center, as if bringing his own spotlight. Nothing short of resplendent in his immaculate white garment. Somehow, he reminds me somehow of Botticelli's famous painting of Venus arising from the ocean, impossibly fresh and pure. (And dry.)

This real-life spiritual teacher doesn't merely sit down, like a visitor in your living room. First, a deerskin is carefully placed over a couch, a sofa that dominates the stage. Then the holy man from India arranges himself there, comfortably cross-legged, his dignity immense, his smile gracious.

Only after he settles in and looks over at his audience do we, as if in a celestial dream, sink down onto our folding chairs. Following that, after giving us one more dollop of glittery pause, Maharishi begins to speak.

Never before have I heard such a musical voice, tender and true. I feel inspiration floating within his every word. Partly I'm listening but mostly I'm singing inside, because of his presence.

The quality of God Here Everywhere Now, of course I recognize this. It is swirling around the room like crazy. That is everywhere, more densely than I have ever heard it before or felt it beneath my feet or tasted it like a deep, ripe bite out of joy-flavored fruit.

Right after the lecture is over, my guru leaves the lecture hall. The rest of us leave as well. As for me, I race up to my room to write a poem about it. Of course. This is why people write poetry.

Early next morning, before our first meeting, I clutch my little poem, which I have copied onto fresh paper in my nicest calligraphy, paper that I've rolled into a sort of improvised scroll.

Carrying this carefully, I run downstairs. Right away I see a dozen students standing outside the stage entrance to the lecture hall, students in a double line that forms a kind of advance walkway for the guru; and for some reason, every one of these people is holding flowers, like a parade straight out of a florist's store.

A tall guy with a sweet smile, probably an initiator who studied with Maharishi in India, walks over to me. He has noticed I have no flower. He explains to me that, according to tradition, you are allowed to give the guru the gift of a flower when he walks by. Then this kindly initiator gives me one of his extra flowers, a white one. Ah!

Sure enough, before entering his lecture hall, Maharishi walks down this very walkway, graciously accepting each person's flower. As he approaches, my heart pounds so hard, I can hardly think or breathe. Yet somehow, I force myself to do exactly what I have been rehearsing to myself ever that kind stranger gave me a flower.

Soon as I hand over my flower, I extend my other hand to present the scrolled-up poem. "And a poem for you, Maharishi," I gasp, in an unfamiliar voice, both shaky and breathless.

The great man stops directly in front of me, his fathomless brown eyes looking straight at me, until I feel as though moving upward way too fast on a cosmic Ferris wheel.

"Read it then," he says.

My inner rehearsal didn't go like this. According to my plan, Maharishi would simply take my paper along with the flower and perhaps read my poem at his convenience. Much later. Maybe never.

Feeling beyond unprepared, of course I can't read him a thing. Just now I could barely utter my well-rehearsed words, "And a poem for you, Maharishi," Now I'm supposed to unfurl my poem and read it like some kind of poet laureate?

Unsurprisingly then, what follows is a mortifying silence in which my body turns incapable of movement, except for how my face blushes like an overripe cherry; and following that, most mortifying of all, my mouth gapes open in a silent stutter of agony.

"Read it in the lecture hall then, so all might hear," Maharishi says lightly, turning to process down the line to his next flower-bringer, and then the next; until deftly gathering up his full bouquet, eventually he enters the lecture hall.

Sitting through that second meeting, I don't hear much except for the guru's chiming presence. Then I go back to my room and cry for two weeks.

Okay, to be accurate, I am also rounding as well, doing my six rounds a day, and as every experienced TMer knows, that means loads of unstressing.

My routine also includes eating fine vegetarian fare in the dining hall and going to each astounding meeting in the lecture hall. Nobody at Brandeis ever taught as Maharishi does: no prepared lectures; no preparation whatsoever, except for his ever-dependable eternal wisdom.

Course participants line up at a microphone, because everyone is allowed to ask questions of the guru. Invariably he responds with the most profound answers, all of which I write down as best I can, arranging his words into iambic pentameter (the meter of a Shakespeare sonnet, which is only fitting).

Mostly, though, during those next two weeks my main deal is crying, because my lifelong passion for writing sure got me into a jam.

Of course, I long to obey my guru and read him that poem, fearlessly read it in front of everyone, as though public speaking were nothing to me. But I have always been a shy person. As a child, meeting strangers, I used to stand in back of my father to hide. By high school I was a notorious wimp when it came to speaking in front of a classroom.

Just how bad was it? Back at U.N.I.S., the one year my class performed a school play (a satire in French by Moliere) I was given a non-speaking role out of kindness for all concerned: the parents in the audience, the teachers who knew me all too well, and especially a certain frantic girl, whose voice would have been shaking so hard that nobody in the audience could have told if I was speaking English or French or choice tidbits from *La Rebellion de Las Masas.*

Accordingly, the pudgy little actress from Flushing made her cameo appearance in a nonspeaking role as the Fencing Master. And now, here in Maine, I'm supposed to stand in front of a microphone and figure out how to talk on a mike for the first time ever? And then read out my poem? Or manage to do anything at all... when I stand in the sacred lecture hall, before an audience of 2,000 people? Plus, my guru!

For sure, I've got a spiritual crush on this man in the white silk dhoti, a crush far bigger than Jimmy Lovelace and Mark Seligson and even Donald, multiplied by the number of moonbeams in the entire galaxy!

However, it's pretty clear that facing down the microphone is the only way I will ever get to give Maharishi that poem.

Eventually, after two weeks, I force myself to stand in line at the microphone, clutching the piece of paper containing my poem. Usually, in my safely anonymous seat, I'd be savoring every word of my beloved guru's discourse.

Only this time, I don't hear a thing. He could be reading us baseball scores and I wouldn't even notice. Incidentally, it's hard to say which I am clenching harder, the sweat-dampened copy of my poem... or my jaws.

Finally, finally, my turn come. I announce that I am going to read a poem. And. Then. I. Read. One. Word. After. Another.

My Guru

When, at last, by Maharishi, I sat down

No effort was needed, none, at last.

"Beautiful," Maharishi says.

My eyes gently watched those liquid stars of his.

No eyelid could dim that forever light.

"Beautiful," Maharishi says.

My lips learned what it is to hold all speech.

What question would not be charmed

By that smile, in fullness formed?

Warmed by the scent of human flesh in flower

My nostrils breathe an ever-deepening joy.

"Beautiful," he says.

What need is there that words be adequate

When there is nothing speech could amplify?

Yet for my own delight, the tinkling chains

of thought-without-an-end

extend

until their bonds are infinite.

Shaking, I stumble back to my seat and sit down. Maharishi has called my poem "Beautiful." And more than once.

I'll save up my tears until I'm safely back in my room; okay, I'll save up most of my tears. Meanwhile, Maharishi is asking the group, "And how many more poets are here?"

To my surprise — or maybe not — hundreds of hands move upward. Some are waving frantically, reminiscent of my hand-raises back in second grade. Maharishi invites us to read out any poems we might have. From now on we can bring them to evening meeting, read our poems at the microphone, along with asking our usual questions for gaining knowledge.

During my last two weeks at the Poland Springs course, I write and read a lot of poems, including this one about what you could call spiritual shyness: the fear of admitting to ourselves how closely connected we might be to God, after all.

Lace

Hold me all in softness.

Let Your breath draw close to me,

O Folder of Rose Petals.

When will I be beauty filled, with Your sumptuous delicacy?

Let me, so I may

unbind the veil that now covers my eyes.

Confused, I cower, shy

to gaze upon Your face that looks at me.

How you who have crocheted me as a lace

must laugh to watch the untangling of this knot.

On the final day of this Teacher Training Part One, while out walking with another woman my age, a bee starts buzzing around. She swats it away dismissively, like a blissful meditator. What happens next? That bee stings *me*, right on the left eyelid.

Who knew that a person could react so strongly to one little bee sting? When it comes time for our final evening lecture, my whole face has swollen up, my left eye completely slammed shut as if trapped beneath a pink-and-fleshy tennis ball of my swollen skin. Taking a glance in the mirror I look pretty darned freaky, but I clutch my farewell poem anyway. With determination.

Reading it aloud at the mike, I try persuading myself that a grotesque appearance simply adds poignancy to my message about overcoming grief. Who wouldn't feel grievously afflicted at having to leave our beautiful, heavenly, Poland Springs hotel? During my culminating poem of the course, Maharishi appears unimpressed, if not outright bored. But I slink back to my seat in the usual way, contenting myself with this thought: "Sometimes folks win at the mike, and sometimes they don't."

Questing Reader, can you guess which person at the microphone wins bigtime? Which person interests Maharishi the most by far, during our month-long course? To answer that one? You don't have to be a Maharishi Mahesh, a Dispeller of Ignorance. There's one obvious winner. Just think "Which man could potentially help my guru far more than anyone else at this TM Teacher Training?"

Someone not famous yet. But sure to become very famous, and soon. I'll never forget the afternoon when our highest-status guest speaker is introduced to us all: Herbert Benson, that's *Doctor* Herbert Benson, mind you. Onstage he speaks to us as if he owns that stage, as if he feels way taller than the man next to him, that insignificant brown man from India.

Holding his microphone, Mr. Herbert Bigshot from Harvard explains that he has been studying TM's physiological effects. Maharishi, a physics major during his college years, always encourages scientific research on TM's benefits, so he beams sunnily as Benson explains to his audience that he's investigating something called a "Relaxation Response."

Unlike Maharishi, I have never cared much for scientific research. Mostly I zone out while Dr. Benson speaks. However, as an English major, I do notice how often Benson makes a verbal distinction between us, the meditators in his audience, and what he calls *normal people.* To me, this sounds remarkably contemptuous.

And do I really hear him *brag* that he hasn't learned Transcendental Meditation? And he smugly tell us that he never wants to, because this might compromise his scientific credibility. Are we supposed to be grateful to this arrogant man, despite his thinly disguised contempt for us all? Honestly! People not in The Movement can be so terribly ignorant.

CHAPTER 30

Officially Becoming a Spiritual Teacher

Corona is a Queens neighborhood that, a few years from now, will be introduced to many through Paul Simon's song, *Me and Julio, Down by the Schoolyard*. Personally, I've never heard of this place until, in the fall of 1970, Donald finds us an apartment there. It's going to be our newlywed's home.

Mom takes me shopping to buy the sweetest little dining table with matching chairs. While my Aunt Ellen splurges on an obviously expensive wedding gift, a gigantic asparagus fern in a gorgeous ceramic flowerpot. Imagine that!

I grew up with no houseplants, have never even seen any (except at my Aunt Ellen's apartment), and now I'm not only married but have been given my very own plant to take care of. Sadly, I have no clue what's required, so over the next few months, I watch it die a long, lingering, yellow-needley sort of death. Perhaps this is related to something I don't really understand very well, something called *watering*.

Most notably, Donald buys his first suit, and when he wears it, standing anywhere in our fabulous new apartment, could any man in all the world be quite so handsome or brilliant?

I'm now living a dream, which is especially amazing since as a child I never had dreams about growing up or living anywhere or marrying anyone or sharing the best spiritual path in the universe with a mystic artist soul man.

Yet here we are, thanks to Grandpa Hugo, since he left each of his four grandchildren an inheritance of $5,000, big money in 1969! That's how I manage tuition for a graduate program at New York University, where I'm majoring in Elementary Education and Dance Education. Meanwhile, Donald has found some job, somewhere. The guy's always amazing at finding a job.

For both of us, the highlight of every week comes when we volunteer at the Manhattan TM Center, where I've begun part-time work as a Meditation Checker.

Checkers help meditators to fine-tune their practice, mostly reminding them to meditate *effortlessly* (which is harder than you might imagine). At the Cambridge TM Center, volunteering as a checker didn't used to seem intimidating, but here in The Big Apple? Oh yes, intimidating.

My first time checking at the sophisticated Manhattan TM Center, I sit in a large room honeycombed into screened-off checking areas. Both my meditator and I may feel equally uncomfortable, although for different reasons. Technically I'm well prepared, having memorized the extremely lengthy and complex checking procedure. (Maharishi's foolproof method is designed like a flowchart). Despite having officially attained status as a *checker*, inwardly my status remains *an insecure mess*.

Providing my first checking session at this TM Center seems to take forever. Soon as I'm done, Susan Seifert taps me on the shoulder and whispers for me to follow. It's an honor talking with her, since she's an experienced initiator, trained in India on the very same course with The Beatles as my own teacher, Terry Gustafson.

After she grabs me by the arm and pulls me into a back room, Susan glares at me with screaming rage in her eyes. However, her voice remains studiously mellow as she asks, "What did you think you were doing?"

After I look at her in bewilderment, Susan continues, "You keep saying 'Relax.' This word is not anywhere in the checking procedure. Besides, you are *screaming* the word 'Relax.' You're screaming so loud, everybody in the entire Center can hear you."

Clearly, this is one more experience to add to my *Life List of Humiliation.* (That's like a birdwatcher's list, only longer.)

But if checking holds terrors for me, that's nothing compared with the other kind of skill required of anyone who aspires to attend Teacher Training Part Two, and thus become one of Maharishi's initiators. Every one of us must learn how to give the Introductory Lecture.

Sorry, no exceptions, definitely no exceptions for shy people who would rather die than to stand in front of an audience for public speaking. At least the Manhattan TM Center encourages us to start lecturing. Every Friday night, we Poland Springs graduates may attend a free class given by glamorous Jack Forem, who is handsome and charismatic, though not nearly so handsome or charismatic as my Donald. Still, Jack will go on to write a national bestseller introducing people to Transcendental Meditation.

During our Lecture Practice events, Jack helps 20 of us learn how to give that oh-so-important free talk about the fastest and best technique ever designed for reaching Enlightenment.

Fortunately, the words we're to use in this speech have also been perfectly designed, thanks to Maharishi. He has given us perfect, standardized, Introductory Lecture-type speeches, brilliantly allowing four different speakers to each cover a single topic.

Actually, these are the very same topics I heard back at my Intro Lecture at Brandeis: Mental Potential, Health, Social Behavior, and World Peace.

Encouragingly, every meeting, Jack asks four students to practice delivering one lecture topic each. Finally, one terrifying Friday night, we last four holdouts must take our turns.

At home I have practiced and practiced, although nothing has dispelled my fear. Meanwhile, brilliant Donald has never practiced, not even once, yet wouldn't you know? When his turn comes, he delivers a perfect version of Mental Potential.

My topic comes soon enough: Social Behavior. While speaking, I read directly from my page of notes. No way will I look up even once to make visual contact with my audience.

> ➢ Does it help that everybody in the room is crazy about TM, just like me?
> ➢ Does it help that, by now, everybody in our group could deliver this Intro Lecture any day, any time, and probably even while dreaming?

No, not the least bit helpful for me. Doggedly I focus on the task at hand and manage to (grimly) deliver all the points about how TM will make you happy and well-adjusted, effective in every social situation, truly popular, etc.

Once my terrifying ordeal is over, finally, I look up. How is my audience reacting?

Every person in the room is shaking, physically shaking. Ooookay.

Nonetheless, Jack Forem informs me that I have now passed Lecturer Training. He is such a kind man. Now Donald and I are allowed to attend Part Two of the TM Teacher Training Course.

Blame those Beatles for what comes next. Although I'm 2/3 of the way through my graduate program, with a master's degree within easy reach, Donald and I happen to hear Paul McCartney's new song on the radio, and we simply can't wait any longer.

The long and winding road

That leads to your door...

Paul has given voice to our greatest longing. We must reach God's door. What urgency we feel, craving to join Maharishi, no more fooling around. Teacher Training now! Enlightenment soon!

Once we decide for sure, all the details work out. Off we head for Mallorca, Spain, spending the last of my inheritance from Grandpa Hugo.

Our first time in Europe, wow! On the ride from the airport, I marvel at how sweet the air smells, although I can't tell, is it the orange groves or the fertilizer? Either way, I adore it.

For three entire days, I can't get that sweet smell out of my nose. Another change is how I start thinking in Spanish a lot of the time. Thank you, Senor Ballada from U.N.I.S. Plus, maybe in the background of my mind I'm kind of hearing how other people are thinking in Spanish. Whatever!

Soon enough, I'm back to thinking 100% in English. That's helpful, since Maharishi gives us lectures (in English) every single night. At the lecture hall we listen attentively. Then we stagger back to the nearby hotels in which we're staying.

Why stagger? When not having meals or sleeping, we're supposed to be rounding, *unlimited rounding*, doing as many rounds as we can manage each day.

Apart from the sparkling Mediterranean, which I can see from my room but never once manage to visit, the landscape of Mallorca turns out to be exactly like the scenery outside my hotel in Poland Springs, Maine.

Okay, one detail is different here, thanks to some fun-loving Spaniards. Questing Reader, picture this. While we spaced-out meditators are walking the couple of blocks to Maharishi's hotel for the evening lecture, who arrives on our street, seemingly out of nowhere?

It's some random driver who races toward us from the opposite direction. Speeding up as his car draws dangerously close to one of us, the driver swerves at the last minute, barely missing the terrified meditator. Then the merry prankster drives away.

How entertainingly we must have jumped! Thus, some *normal people* from the land of bullfighting entertain themselves with these unusually ridiculous tourists -- the slowest-walking, most glassy-eyed, blissfully smiling hippies in the entire history of India. (Joke. I mean, the history of Mallorca.)

Of course, Maharishi completely makes up for the nuisance of those obnoxious drivers, and he also makes up for the dreadful food in our hotel restaurant.

Among other dishes, every night we are served from an immense platter of Brussels sprouts slathered in garlic. (This vegetable lover won't stomach eating another Brussels sprout for at least 12 years.)

Really, though, who cares? Maharishi's presence and wisdom enchant me. Also, the greatest pandits from India are staying with us, chanting from a Hindu scripture called the *Rig Veda*, recording their performances onto audiotapes so that other meditators can listen later, even if they're not fortunate enough to witness the live performances that we get to hear.

Among these singers of ancient words, impossible to understand, but with soul-stirring intensity; the pandit I notice most is the oldest man I've ever seen, Brahmarishi Devarata, with a curvy nose and bristling white eyebrows, as if his face has been carved out of ancient stone cliffs that will always endure.

Even while singing so vigorously, he gives me the feeling that inwardly he's somehow not moving at all. Since the pandit doesn't speak much English, we never hear him talk, only sing. Adding to Devarata's allure, we've been told that his consciousness is exceptional. Maharishi says that this holy singer has a really advanced kind of Enlightenment, a high state of God Consciousness.

And even if I didn't always believe every single word from my guru, which of course I do, Brahmarishi Devarata's eyes would convince me: eyes as lively as a powerful waterfall cascading beneath ancient cliffs. This man must be really, amazingly, spiritually awake.

Apart from the Vedic chanting, and all of Maharishi's wisdom during the lectures, what else do I absolutely adore about our evening meetings? Right before our meeting ends, every single night, our guru leads the assembled group in singing the *puja* (pronounced POO-jaah), the ceremony used during TM initiations.

This sacred music stirs my heart every time, a sacredness gaining power from all the voices in our large group. It's a mysterious sacredness from words in the ancient language of Vedic Sanskrit. Maharishi has taught us the meaning of all these words. Especially I love this part:

Akhanda-mandalakaram vyaptam yena characharam.

Like the unbounded canopy of the sky,

pervading everything in creation.

Although I can't imagine what it would be like to experience in Guru Dev's way, I just love those words. They make me think, "Bigger than All the Night Sky."

While instructing us in the puja, Maharishi has explained the meaning of every word. Yet what has our guru failed to mention? What Donald noticed so clearly during his initiation, how that song causes a full parade of Holy Tradition gurus to walk straight into the room.

I guess everybody else on Teacher Training is clairvoyant like Donald, so all of them watch this nightly parade fill up our lecture hall, with all this glory being far too obvious (and also too sacred) for them to discuss in front of me.

During this Teacher Training Course, I'm must be missing so much. Especially when I hear others share their experiences in meditation, it's pathetically obvious that I'm kind of a dud.

At least I have a chance to improve, because here we're allowed to do as many rounds as possible, not just 2 per day, like at home; or 6, like on a regular residence course; but as many as we can. One day I even manage to squeeze in 15 full sets of meditate-asanas-pranayama.

The only downside to all that rounding is the unstressing. Here in Mallorca, I'm releasing stress even more than at Poland Springs, with my latest fears centered around flunking out of this Teacher Training. Why would Maharishi ever consider me worthy to become a spiritual teacher?

Me, so insecure and neurotic. Although no longer a teenager, I still have pimples, for crying out loud. How can I ever, possibly, ever, be good enough to represent The Movement?

One afternoon, unstressing away, I'm crying harder than usual, sobbing as if my ribs will break, sobbing so hard that I have to stop meditating, sobbing even after I lie down and try to take a nap.

Somehow, I feel Donald enter the room in a spirit body. He gives me a hug, then leaves.

Of course, we are sleeping in separate rooms here. On a Residence Course, you're not allowed to mess up your energies with sex. But I'm allowed to eat with Donald at mealtimes, so at dinner I ask him what happened that afternoon.

Before today I never even knew that people had spirit bodies, let alone being able to fly around in one, just to give your wife a desperately needed hug.

"You don't know how to do that?" Donald says, looking at me funny. Once again, I am awed by my super-evolved husband. At least I'm evolving as fast as I can, thanks to all that rounding.

Sometimes my experiences in meditation are beautiful, but what really keeps me going is the knowledge that stress release leads directly to Enlightenment.

Also consoling, I write some new poems for Maharishi, reading them at evening meetings. Always, I read my new poems to him soon after writing them. Despite shaking with fear, at least I've learned to ignore the group and the microphone.

Also, it helps that I never lift my eyes from the page until the reading is over. Following that, sometimes I'll steal one quick glance at the white-robed man sitting on his deerskin… as if on a cloud. Fast as I can, I race back to my seat.

One memorable time, I approach the microphone with another new poem written just for my guru. This one I introduce, explaining, "Maharishi, this poem is called *Fealty*, which is a kind of loyalty oath that people in Europe would make in the Middle Ages."

Fealty

Why is it that this night, while all of nature sleeps,

my eyes open in joy after each blink?

My window overlooks a town whose doors and roofs

all blanketed in peace rest silently,

While inside this small house I sit and smile.

Today after long miles of journeying

a wooden staff my only company

I reached the iron gate, passed the stone wall

and did not stop until, in the great hall

where the red carpet reaches to the throne,

I kneeled. I searched for words that would explain

how I would lay my life down for my king.

I did not dare to look. My calloused palms outstretched,

how many years did I spend in that pain?

When with his royal voice he suddenly beseeched

some words with which I might him entertain.

Like a young child whose tongue begins to babble speech

and lo, his words are heard for the first time,

Thus, I did find my tale, spoken so recklessly...

brought joy to my lord who owns everything.

My simple life, of cloth woven for daily wear,

brought pleasure to his silken majesty.

So, I may come again

and then again return.

So long as stories can be spoken, shall I speak.

May my sight be so full

that there be endless fuel

to burn in the warm hearth of my dear king.

Soon as the last word is uttered, I hand over my microphone to the next person in line. Then I walk back to my seat. Although still shaking a bit, mostly I'm relieved to have managed to read every word, and do that without dying of embarrassment.

Gratefully I duck back to my chair, next to Blaine. She's a girl my age. Over the last few months, I've managed to not exchange a single word with her. Questing Reader, why achieve that perfect record? Because Blaine intimidates me. Basically, in her presence, I feel wormy and intimidated.

The young woman is beautiful, with a flawless complexion (this being something I always notice). Plus, she's dating an initiator named Lincoln, who also appears to be the ultimate in good-looking, verging on glamorous. And even though such things are never discussed in our oh-so-spiritual TM culture, both Blaine and Lincoln are probably quite wealthy.

Relieved that I got through reading my poem, I gaze down at my lap. So many intense feelings roil my emotions, and that includes being dazzled by Blaine's gorgeous slacks, seen out the corner of my eye as I look down toward my own lap. Soft and perfectly tailored are her slacks, made of exquisite wool, and colored a most unusual shade of umber. People like her on this course are so totally out of my league.

This Blaine nudges my shoulder gently, starting to talk to me, and her voice isn't stuck up but kind. Speaking to me for the first time ever since I set foot in Mallorca, months ago, she whispers, "Did you see Maharishi's face when you read out that poem?"

"Of course not," I mutter, now staring fixedly at the floor in front of my feet.

"I thought maybe not," Blaine says tactfully. "Well, let me tell you. You know what happened when you read Maharishi that poem? He cried."

* * *

Questing Reader, you never know when life will deliver you a moment that unexpectedly beautiful!

Most beautiful of all (maybe also a miracle), Maharishi does agree to make me an initiator. In the final portion of Teacher Training, I luck out amazingly, because my charter flight is a small group of 15. We're scheduled to leave Mallorca ahead of the main group, so we will receive training one-on-one, being individually instructed by Maharishi in a small hotel room. And thus, I find myself waiting, standing alone in a long hallway, standing outside a closed door. Having dressed up for the occasion, in the same clothes as on my wedding day, I'm wearing my Marimekko striped skirt, my sunrise yellow blouse, and those perky round earrings.

While I wait, Brahmarishi Devarata walks by. To my astonishment, his head jerks around to look at me. Guess he's noticing me with his peripheral vision. Seriously, I cannot fathom what is going on with this legendary pandit's expanded awareness. And never in an eternity of years could I have guessed what would happen next.

This walking embodiment of the Rig Veda changes direction, moving until he stands directly in front of me, less than one arm's length away. Then this man... who looks to me like a mountain... appears startled, as if seeing something in me that I sure don't see in myself, because then he gestures wide, wide with his arms fully extended, and says expressively, in his uncomfortable English, "Big!!!!"

That said, he simply goes on his way, turning away and continuing his walk down the hallway. He's walking, really, like any normal man who happens to look and move and sound like a mountain.

Puzzled, I wonder if he has just given my aura the greatest compliment of my life, or maybe this is simply how Vedic pandits talk to any random strangers they pass in a hallway, or maybe he speaks this way only to people who are waiting to be made TM initiators.

Abruptly my time for wondering ends as the door to Maharishi's room opens. And opens by his very own hand! Eyes wide, I enter the room to receive my initiator's initiation.

Maharishi reaches over to close the door, then seats himself on an ordinary folding chair. No sitting in lotus position this time! Somehow, I don't quite believe that he can do such a thing as to sit on a regular chair. Next, as if in a dream, I'm sitting in the only other chair in the room, not exactly feeling normal myself although probably looking normal-ish. As I face him there's just a small card table between us.

Using a turquoise felt-tipped pen, Maharishi writes down all the TM mantras. He tells me how to pronounce each one, then gives me instructions for which mantra to choose for which kind of initiate. Then the greatest man in my world coaches me until I can pronounce each mantra properly.

Ever efficient, he signals that we are done. By now my head feels like a cross between a treasure chest laden with jewels, and a surreal globe about the size of a universe and, also, a clunky skull that contains a couple of human eyes that are staring... because they have forgotten how to blink. Somehow, I manage to stumble out of that room.

Lucky for me, no bullfight-style car happens to drive on the road just then, as I stagger-walk back to my hotel. If one of those fun-loving Spaniards tried razzing me, I might pass out. Or get run over. Or fly straight up to the heavens.

* * *

Hours later, my group of 15 is sitting in our chartered bus, speeding us all to the Mallorca Airport. All of us squeaky new initiators appear somewhat dazed, and why wouldn't we?

Between the months of rounding and now our intense gratitude, having just received sacred knowledge directly from Maharishi; and although we never, ever want to leave him, obediently we're riding our bus to the airport, where we will catch a flight from Mallorca to Madrid. All goes as planned, and soon I'm with our small group of 15, disembarked from our first plane and now walking toward the second, a long flight that will take us from Madrid to New York.

Walking through the terminal in Madrid, we're forced to stop for a moment. Evidently two much larger crowds are crossing in front of us, each crowd coming from a different direction.

While waiting for the larger of these two groups to pass, I stare at the smaller group of tourists, which happens to be stuck directly in front of me. Faster than I can think, "I am having an experience," what happens? I see all the people in that crowd. I mean, I really see them.

Shockingly, they're the first group of non-blissy, normal people that I have encountered in three months, but what's even more shocking? How oddly I am seeing them!

Because somehow each person stands illuminated, as if through a celestial spotlight that lovingly shines down from above, sweetly lighting up each face. So beautiful these strangers look, each one adorable as a clean, happy baby. Only there's more to see, and do I ever see it! That glowing spotlight also reveals each person's pain.

How can I be feeling this pain? Me, of all people? Me, acknowledging pain! For most of my life as Laura, I have done anything and everything to avoid seeing anybody's pain; for instance, defending myself against seeing my parents' pain (which could have been just as visible to me as their physical nakedness around the apartment).

Like that, I've studiously ignored most of my sister's pain, although she had an even harder time growing up than I did; including those months in elementary school when Amy used to walk around carrying a kind of prop wherever she went out in public. You see, Questing Reader, Amy insisted on carrying around – like a street sign -- a book by Dostoyevsky called *The House of the Dead.*

And especially I've avoided noticing my own fears and pain, doing a kind of disappearing act on myself; avoiding conscious recognition of pain whenever possible, determined to never wallow in self-pity like my mother.

Well, here it is now, just the opposite of my usual way of living, with All Pain Locked Inside. Something I never knew existed, and never would have chosen to find -- for this long moment I am seeing dozens of people in their full spiritual glory, and also in their very enormous personal pain.

Strangers are paused right in front of me, under this mysterious spotlight that reveals spiritual truth, and I have no choice but to face each stranger, looking at each one in turn, but not blissfully as Ram Dass might have done.

No, I'm viewing them humanly, perhaps more willing to notice humans than ever I've been, except for one time long ago, leaping down from the ceiling of a Manhattan hospital room, and squeezing myself into a squirming animal body... so that I could be born.

In that Madrid airport hallway, it's as though time will not progress until I have agreed to notice the humanity of each person in front of me, almost as if that person's guts are hanging out; only what I see is even more personal than body parts, and just as real as a heart or a liver, because I'm seeing each soul's patterns of fear and anger, sorrow and hopelessness.

Never before have I let myself feel how perfectly normal-looking people could carry so much inner pain: unremitting pain. Although that pain is worse for some than for others, every single one of these strangers carries so much misery, walling them off from other humans, and intensifying a terrible quality of aloneness, *Earth alone.*

Recognize pain? Who, me? For months, pushing myself to do as many rounds as possible, often pausing to sob uncontrollably but proudly uninterested in my mere feelings, explaining them all away as a kind of meaningless, generic unstressing.

Rounding away, despite so many tears, I didn't even feel my deepest pain of all, treating it instead like a bunch of ideas. Yet I had felt shame, believing myself utterly unworthy to ever become a spiritual teacher.

Now I'm being given this unsought show-and-tell, all about how other people suffer, too... and including how much emotional pain I have felt... and yet all these strangers have suffered at least as much as I have... hurting inside, whether they consciously knew it or not.

Shaken, I inwardly call out to God.

Yes, I see it now, this terrible suffering.

Please, make me a real teacher. Help me to make a real difference.

And I promise you, I won't care if I look like a fool and people make fun of me.

I won't mind if I keep having pimples, or whatever else.

All that matters is this: Let me help them. Make me good enough to really help them.

Afterword

The night sky is just one of life's big mysteries, isn't it? Mysteries of mine include that Narnia-like hidden passageway in my closet, a mystery I later read about in novels by C.S. Lewis but, personally, never have solved.

However, Questing Reader, later in this lifetime I've managed to solve other mysteries that you have read about here -- although at the time, they never seemed to me like mysteries at all. Only many decades later, certain details of my life that I've shared with you here — only later would these *become* mysteries that I'd wonder about and, eventually, even solve.

> ➤ Like how my awkward moment in ballet class hinted at something lovely, like a Divine game of peek-a-boo.

> ➤ Or why it happened, while sleeping over at Grandma Gisela's apartment, my eyes became so frighteningly glued together.

> ➤ Or why so many of the confusions in my early life were related to a word I wouldn't learn until I was in my forties: Empath. Here, Questing Reader, you've seen a portrait of a very unskilled empath.

> ➤ Other mysteries involved my guru at the time, including multiple reasons why Maharishi would unwittingly bring me a very personal kind of heartbreak.

> ➤ Also, I discovered surprises (and mystery) concerning my fealty to my guru, a loyalty which wouldn't last. And couldn't. And didn't.

> ➢ However, Maharishi prepared me to live a different kind of fealty, a hard kind, yet the most fulfilling kind imaginable.

Perhaps, in the future, I'll have a chance to tell you those stories of mine, Questing Reader. Perhaps, someday, you'll tell me stories, too. I'd like that.

About the Author

Since this is a memoir, Questing Reader, let's have some fun with author photos. Here I am, a couple of years before this memoir ends.

And here I am now, as someone who improbably became the founder of Energy Spirituality®, someone who gets to help clients and teach online workshops, and even write a memoir.

Questing Readers

Fear and trembling… Before publishing this memoir, I believed that big-time fear and trembling were for lofty philosophers like Søren Kierkegaard, not the likes of me. Well, preparing this memoir has dunked me into emotions like these. Compared to other kinds of writing that I've published? Sharing this memoir feels way more close-to-the bone, so inescapably personal.

Now, with the completion of this book, I'm starting a new phase with its own special kinds of vulnerability. *The book review phase.*

Questing Reader, when you're an indie publisher like me, it can be really hard to get book reviews. Maybe you know already that the publishing establishment turns up its nose at self-published books like mine, won't even look at them. For that reason, I'm asking for your help.

Please write a review of this book, then share it at Amazon.com, goodreads.com, and any other book review opportunities you encounter. Even a couple of sentences can make such a difference, spreading the word about a memoir that was created in a manner that was heartfelt but decidedly not glamorous.

This Big Fancy Publisher works in a little pink office in Sterling, Virginia. That is, my workplace is a small upstairs bedroom in a small house. Hey, I can see why *Publishers Weekly* isn't impressed by the likes of me.

But if this book has moved you or helped you, it could be simple for you to write a sentence or more, reviewing this memoir. Seems like, if this book is to reach many people, it will have to be due to word of mouth and online book reviews. So, if you're game, please help. You're invited to email me afterward so that I can thank you personally. It's roserosetree@verizon.net.

More Books by Rose Rosetree

SERIES 1. Energy READING Skills

BOOK 1. *The NEW Power of Face Reading*
Face Reading Secrets® helps you to improve communication, gain more self-esteem.

BOOK 2. *Aura Reading Through All Your Senses*
Over 100 practical applications are yours, along with insight into your personal gifts for energetic literacy.

BOOK 3. *Read People Deeper*
Body Language + Face Reading + Auras = fascinating insights into power, sex, truthfulness, and more. Great for online dating!

SERIES 2: Energy HEALING Skills

BOOK 1. *Use Your Power of Command for Spiritual Cleansing*
Really Effective Skills for energetic decluttering.

BOOK 2. *Cut Cords of Attachment for SELF-HEALING*
Learn the real deal, 12 Steps to Cut Cords of Attachment®.

BOOK 3. *The New Strong*
Stop fixing yourself — and actually accelerate your personal growth! Rules and tools for thriving in the Age of Awakening.

SERIES 3: Empath Empowerment® Books

BOOK 1. *Empath Empowerment in 30 Days*
BECOME A Skilled Empath in just 15 minutes a day.

BOOK 2. *The Empowered Empath: Quick & Easy*

The first book to describe what happens during subconscious Split-Split-Second Empath Merges, offering highly effective techniques to end these habits.

BOOK 3. *The Empowered Empath: Expanded Edition*

Learn even more about owning, embracing, and managing your special empath gifts.

BOOK 4. *The Master Empath*

Learn ways to do "Skilled Empath Merge." Each time you can *purposely* experience what it is like to be someone else — directly, powerfully, clearly, safely.

SERIES 4: Enlightenment Coaching Books

BOOK 1. *Seeking Enlightenment in the Age of Awakening*

Never before have you had the chance to explore a program like this, an up-to-date and effective Program for Spiritual Enlightenment that works now, after the end of the Age of Faith.

BOOK 2. *Let Today Be a Holiday*

This spiritual daybook offers 365 ways to co-create with God.

BOOK 3. *Magnetize Money with Energetic Literacy*

Ten secrets for success and prosperity can help you to make more money. Also, learn how to develop a "consciousness lifestyle" that's worthy of you; you can gain many new concepts to help you grow emotionally and evolve spiritually, now that we're living in the Age of Awakening.

Enjoy "Free Tastes" of all Rose's books.
Browse at https://www.rose-rosetree.com/books/